The International Network of Principals' Centers

The International Network of Principals' Centers sponsors *New Directions for School Leadership* as part of its commitment to strengthening leadership at the individual school level through professional development for leaders. The Network has a membership of principals' centers, academics, and practitioners in the United States and overseas and is open to all groups and institutions committed to the growth of school leaders and the improvement of schools. The Network currently functions primarily as an information exchange and support system for member centers in their efforts to work directly with school leaders in their communities. Its office is in the Principals' Center at the Harvard Graduate School of Education.

The Network offers these services:

- The International Directory of Principals' Centers features member centers with contact persons, descriptions of center activities, program references, and evaluation instruments.
- The Annual Conversation takes place every spring, when members meet for seminars, workshops, speakers, and to initiate discussions that will continue throughout the year.
- *Newsnotes*, the Network's quarterly newsletter, informs members of programs, conferences, workshops, and special interest items.
- *Reflections*, an annual journal, includes articles by principals, staff developers, university educators, and principals' center staff members.

For further information, please contact:

International Network of Principals' Centers
Harvard Graduate School of Education
336 Gutman Library
Cambridge, MA 02138
(617) 495-9812

NO. 9, FALL 1998

NEW DIRECTIONS FOR SCHOOL LEADERSHIP

Conceptual and Practical Issues in School Leadership

Insights and Innovations from the U.S. and Abroad

REBECCA VAN DER BOGERT
Winnetka Public Schools, Evanston, Illinois
EDITOR-IN-CHIEF

VIVIAN WILLIAMS
St. Peter's College, University of Oxford, England
EDITOR

CONCEPTUAL AND PRACTICAL ISSUES IN SCHOOL LEADERSHIP:
INSIGHTS AND INNOVATIONS FROM THE U.S. AND ABROAD
Vivian Williams (ed.)
New Directions for School Leadership, No. 9, Fall 1998
Rebecca van der Bogert, Editor-in-Chief

ISSN 1089-5612   ISBN 0-7879-4274-X

NEW DIRECTIONS FOR SCHOOL LEADERSHIP is part of The Jossey-Bass Education Series and is published quarterly by Jossey-Bass Inc., Publishers, 350 Sansome Street, San Francisco, California 94104-1342.

SUBSCRIPTIONS: Please see Back Issue/Subscription Order Form at the end of the journal.

EDITORIAL CORRESPONDENCE should be sent to Rebecca van der Bogert, Winnetka Public Schools, 1235 Oak Street, Winnetka, Illinois 60093.

Jossey-Bass Web address: www.josseybass.com

Printed in the United States of America on acid-free recycled paper containing 100 percent recovered waste paper, of which at least 20 percent is postconsumer waste.

Contents

Foreword

IN A CHAPTER on the twentieth century, Edmund King, the doyen of an international group of writers and researchers in comparative education during the second half of this century, perceptively asserts that one emerging contemporary pattern of social evolution is "putting more emphasis on sharing, on judgement and on concern. At least a triangular relationship is implied between theory, practical knowledge or experience and social insight. In this context the characteristic relationship is one of learning and helping to learn. . . . Knowledge and understanding are continuously built in a co-operative enterprise" (Boyd and King, 1995).

This is an entirely appropriate context for this journal, which is devoted to leadership studies from an international perspective. Throughout this issue, the central theme is organizational and cultural change requiring collaborative leadership in recently developed systems of self-managing schools, focusing on schools in England and Wales and Israel. Other contributions from colleagues in U.S. schools serve to underline that irrespective of systemic frameworks, the essence of effective leadership is embedded in collective, interprofessional, shared commitment to educational development.

In the first international issue of this journal, the central objective has been to introduce readers to the universality of educational concepts, issues, dilemmas, and achievements of colleagues in other countries. The selection is demonstrably eclectic and represents an attempt to provide a collection of innovative developments at a variety of scales: national, regional, community, and school-based. As the themes are concerned with increasing school autonomy, the

NEW DIRECTIONS FOR SCHOOL LEADERSHIP, NO. 9, FALL 1998 © JOSSEY-BASS PUBLISHERS

pivotal role of headteachers and principals who *earn* their leadership authority is self-evident. The leadership focus is clearly moving away from earlier static conceptions of positional leadership to more dynamic and ultimately more fulfilling status earned from colleagues as the "leading professional" within collaborative school cultures.

The significance of perceptions of change at the international level is emphasized through the nature of the editor's invitation to contributors to this issue. As leaders, all authors have experience as visitors to school systems overseas. They were asked to frame their contributions through topics that were personally stimulating either as achievements to be shared or as matters of salient concern. Similarly, authors were also invited to share reports on recent leadership research, organizational reform, or cultural change in schools.

A notable feature of the responses has been the ways in which three main themes of international interest have arisen. The first theme is focused on practitioner leadership in a school in England and on initiatives within a group of schools in the Pittsburgh area undergoing curricular and cultural change. It is instructive to note that although the agendas are dissimilar, there are clear similarities that underpin collaborative relationships in successful innovative practice. Second, issues of moral leadership in schools are provided in chapters contributed independently by authors from England and Pennsylvania. Each presents difficult if not entirely intractable dilemmas for schools. Third, interesting parallels arise between accounts of changing leadership culture in response to systemic reforms stemming from the development of site-based management policies for elementary schools in Israel and a research study of a group of reorganized primary schools in England in response to nationally mandated local management of schools.

One contribution is about the universality of emerging theoretical concepts about leadership—hitherto largely neglected in the management literature. These are concepts inherent in notions of *followership*—potentially a highly controversial issue as they require fundamental dismantling of authority exclusively derived from positional status and hallowed by many adherents to the received leadership tradition.

Finally, it is hoped that this volume will be the precursor to other editions in the sharing of issues, developments, and achievements and celebration of the leadership of schools on a global basis—we have much to learn from each other.

Reference

Boyd, W., and King, E. J. *The History of Western Education.* (12th ed.). Lanham, Md.: Barnes & Noble Books, 1995.

VIVIAN WILLIAMS *is fellow in education, St. Peter's College, University of Oxford, director of the Norham Centre for Leadership Studies, and a research fellow of The Leverhulme Trust.*

Derived from analysis of data from schools in the United Kingdom, this chapter explores relationships between leaders and followers. A preliminary typology of followers provides insights into a much-neglected area for collaborative relationships between leaders and followers in professional contexts.

1

Leader and follower relationships: Emerging perceptions about the conceptual nature of followership in education

Vivian Williams

IN RECENT YEARS, leadership theory and research has been an increasingly active concern throughout sociopolitical organizations in a search for more effective and efficient outcomes. Many authors have made notable general contributions. For example, Bennis and Nanus (1985), Burns (1978), Covey (1990), Drucker (1980), Kouzes and Posner (1995), Mintzberg (1979), Peters and Waterman (1982), Senge (1990), and White, Hodgson, and Crainer (1996) have contributed much to the general understanding of the nature and process of leadership. Specifically in education, recent perceptions about the nature of leadership in educational contexts have been offered by several authors, including Barth (1990), Fullan (1991), Johnson (1990), Lieberman (1988), Sergiovanni (1992), Weick (1983), and Williams (1989).

Within and beyond education, these and other authors largely agree that the basis of modern leadership thought and practice rests

NEW DIRECTIONS FOR SCHOOL LEADERSHIP, NO. 9, FALL 1998 © JOSSEY-BASS PUBLISHERS

on perceptions that leadership comprises, and reflects interpersonal processes among people and is not simply the acquisition of appointed hierarchical status or a bundle of discrete managerial skills. In schools as in other professionally staffed organizations, an understanding of leadership requires recognition of a culture that is different from other organizations (Lieberman, 1988; Williams, 1995) in that the value system, symbolism, personal authority, and ownership within loosely structured working arrangements and sense of purpose for collective outcomes are shared among those engaged in educational processes (Barth, 1990; Johnson, 1990; Sergiovanni, 1992; Weick, 1983).

These concepts are partly attributable to an understanding of transformational leadership developed in the seminal work of Burns (1978) and to more recent insights involved in the development of headteachers and principals as "professional leaders." Professional leaders recognize the existence of indissoluble partnerships with collaborative colleagues who elect to undertake a variety of leadership roles as positive contributors in the life and work of schools as communities of learners working toward achievement of holistic educational objectives.

Leadership within school management practice

Recent research suggests that traditional attitudes to leadership are in serious need of revision. There is a sense that earlier views of leaders who conveyed a sense of intellectual superiority, wisdom, and greater executive power than others are no longer automatically accepted. Some authors assert that with the changing requirements in organizations—the demonstrable rejection of the myth of the "great person," personal autonomy, more loosely structured work organization, technical complexity, and greater variety of tasks—together with a reduction in the numerical size of the workforce has increased the perception of self-worth among employees.

These developments have placed a premium on recent interpretations and styles of leadership. *Managing* and *leading* are *not* interchangeable terms. The status, power, and authority in managing or leading activities are derived from different sources. In the activity of management, status, power, and authority are derived essentially from the designated organizational position of the holder of the appointment. These are commonly seen in the relationships between hierarchical positions, the degree of control over others, and the line accountability defined in job descriptions and delineated through organizational rules and procedures. Frequently—and especially in education—it is also linked with stable, tenured positions. However, in the activity of leading there is no direct link with formal status, designated appointment, or the authority of office. Leadership rests on "the power to influence the thinking and behaviour of others to achieve *mutually* desired objectives. . . . Earned leadership is an accorded status not an appointed one. Crucially, in education leadership effectiveness rests on an umbilical relationship between leaders and followers: the voluntary acquiescence of followers has to be *earned* by leaders" (Williams, 1989).

Both managing and leading are essentially activities that depend on relationships with others. The very different processes reflect the perceptions of the people who are involved: "The essential understanding . . . is a simple one, but often overlooked or ignored: that leaders cannot exist without followers" (Williams, 1989). Thus in managing there is a designated positional relationship dependent on differentiated formal status. The relationship is amenable to an impersonal, prescriptive, task-achievement requirement for conformity focused on rewards for compliance and sanctions for non-cooperation. It is a controlling relationship resting on the relative positional status of managers and subordinates.

Earned leadership: Professionalism in school management

Contrastingly, without the requirement of formal status, the leader-follower relationship is always dependent on the willing acquiescence of the followers arising from a continuous two-way interactive process. Leadership power and authority are earned from elective followers—sometimes through the vision offered by the leader but more prosaically in organizations through patient negotiation involving the perceived needs of followers for recognition of value, positive contribution, and commitment to the enterprise, as well as for personal job satisfaction and growth in the undertaking of tasks with the leader's support.

Many managers and leaders in all kinds of organizations including schools use both positional and earned authority in their daily activities. Many do so intuitively but others exercise positional authority in ways that are inappropriate in professionally staffed organizations. Frequently, the latter approach arises from an absence of a clear perception of the fundamental differences between managing and leading colleagues. Such failures are generally attributable to an inability to understand the quality of relationships required for leadership effectiveness: not only for enhancing personal status but, more important, to secure cooperative and unequivocal support of others in undertaking tasks required to achieve declared objectives.

As teachers in schools share largely homogeneous backgrounds by virtue of academic achievement, espoused educational values, and professional commitment to the development of pupils, the more attractive paradigm is the leadership one. Those who hold managerial positions in schools may occupy more senior designated appointments but few could legitimately claim possession of superior intelligence, wisdom, experience, or qualifications than many of their colleagues. Even fewer would be able to demonstrate such "superior" virtues. Distinctive general homogeneity among practitioners clearly indicates that schools require the application of leadership principles to achieve their goals.

Further, in anticipation of emerging school cultures (for example, site-based, self-managing), it is asserted here that leading rather than managing a collective enterprise will, or should, provide *the* natural organizational framework. In these ways, and for those who so wish, opportunities for teachers to share in formulating holistic school development policy, determining teaching and learning strategies, setting staff development priorities, and promoting acceptance of personal accountability for educational outcomes are appropriate activities for collective leadership. Similarly, practitioners with specific expertise who exercise degrees of responsibility for budgetary control, in-school administration, or promoting the school's reputation within its community should participate fully in collaborative and earned leader-follower relationships.

Leaders and followers: Shared professional relationships

A sense of collective purpose has always been a distinctive feature in many successful schools. Recent studies and research have illuminated ways in which this development can be taken beyond an intuitive and random existence.

Traditionally, management literature about school leadership has focused primarily on the position of one person—the institutional leader. Many widely read authors focus on the requirements of the positional leader's role as visionary, innovator, and strategist. Although increasingly obsolescent, the elitist tradition of the "great person" endures—much of it dependent on patriotic interpretations of "heroes" of political and military history, classical literary mythology, and Hollywood film epics. However, during the past half-century or so, biographies of many so-called great persons have revealed major flaws in the notion of superhuman powers possessed by individual leaders together with instances of subsequent disastrous effects arising from the behavior of positional leaders who came to believe they were beyond human frailty.

In education, many teachers who respect and admire their school leaders would find it difficult to adduce leadership characteristics commonly listed in standard management texts. They are more likely to be at ease with the Peters and Waterman (1982) view of leadership as "patient, usually boring coalition building. . . . It is altering agendas so that new priorities get enough attention. It is being visible when things are going awry and invisible when they are working well. It's listening carefully much of the time, frequently speaking with encouragement, and reinforcing words with believable action. It's being tough when necessary and it's the occasional use of naked power—or the 'subtle accumulation of nuances, a hundred things done a little better,' as Henry Kissinger once put it" (p. 82).

Burns (1978) and others emphasize that leaders and followers must combine in the shaping of collective purpose. Interaction between leaders and followers leads to clearer understanding of objectives, mutual needs, and motives than if they act separately. Thus objectives emerge that both are committed to and that, in turn, lead to development in social relations through shared activities required to achieve agreed goals.

It is through the realization that being a leader is not a property or activity but consists of a complex set of *relationships* with followers leading to a merging of mutual purpose, needs, motives, and activities that recent concepts of the role have become clarified. Linked with this clarification is a crucial awareness that followers are not necessarily either sheep or apprentice leaders. For most teachers, the daily reality is that although explicit recognition as leaders may be formally absent, they take initiatives, make intelligent decisions, employ value judgments, and are self-motivated for the benefit of pupils, their colleagues, and the school community. In doing so, they are undertaking the essential tasks as "collaborative colleagues" (Williams, 1995) in the completion of organizational work. This more recent interpretation of the term *follower* leads to the perception of relationships with leaders as one of collegial partnership working toward agreed collective goals. Thus, in education, leading and following are professionally interdependent and essentially complementary and not competitive roles and, significantly, interchangeable according to specific expertise and circumstances.

A key insight that is important to both leaders and followers is an understanding of the circumstances under which people elect to follow others. As yet the process is imperfectly understood, but followership clearly reflects personal considerations and wishes. It is unacceptably simplistic to assume that leaders can persuade others to follow through personal leadership, charisma, or vision. In the author's current research into relationships between leaders and followers, it is becoming clear that many potential teacher-followers distrust charisma and are unattracted by someone else's vision that they have not helped to shape. Others are motivated by their own personal perceptions of ways in which they wish to contribute. These personal considerations represent deliberate choices not simply about careers but also about the quality and rewards of living a life compatible with personality and at ease with oneself.

It is important to recognize that many teachers *choose* to be followers not because of perceived inadequacies but because they make deliberate, considered, and rational choices based on personal preferences. School leaders who recognize, respect, and value their colleagues learn to engage the talents, skills, and experience of these "elective followers"—thereby gaining a wide range of benefits to the collective effort and expressing personal recognition of the value of their contribution to success in the organization.

However, and unlike the published emphasis on leadership types and styles, the relatively novel concept of the importance of elective followership raises problems of recognizing the existence of those who are not traditional stereotypes—sheep, compliants, sycophants, or acolytes. Mintzberg's belief (1979) that the effectiveness of a manager is dependent on the degree of personal insight into the requirements of role is equally applicable to concepts of followership.

Although not fully developed in 1985, an assertion by Bennis and Nanus that effective leadership would become more visible in organizations, "able to respond to spastic and turbulent conditions" (p. 18), was prescient and underlined the centrality of professionally shared responsive leadership in schools. Schools in many countries, including the United Kingdom, are experiencing processes of discontinuous change. Significantly, and in response to the pressures of innovation, organizational models based on positional power are gradually being replaced by new concepts of leadership focused on collective purpose and earned authority. These concepts are of considerable interest to those school leaders who are aware that no hard research evidence exists that demonstrates a positive correlation between designated status and competence in education. Nevertheless, there is a persistent belief that many schools are overmanaged and underled.

However, societal change is universally influential. Unsurprisingly, teachers reflect and in turn are affected by those changes. Just as society has become less tractable in accepting the authority of positional power, teachers' attitudes have moved in similar directions. Adoption of contemporary values, expectations of independent thought and action, challenges to institutional authority, developed self-esteem, and demands to become active contributors in decision-making mechanisms have replaced traditional perceptions of teachers as conformists, uncomplainingly diligent and respectful of positional status. The central task for school leaders is to recognize and accept the realities of these organizational and cultural changes and to see them as positive opportunities to release the energies and engage the considerable talents of elective followers.

The legitimacy of these changing relationships is not a difficult concept to grasp. However, accepting the practical implications of the reality of new relationships has proved to be difficult to achieve in many schools. Although it is relatively easy to devise new structures, it is considerably more difficult to develop positive attitudes to successful organizational change.

New relationships between leaders and followers

It is perhaps superfluous to underline that schools consist of professionally qualified graduates who work within interdependent controlled arrangements to achieve collective objectives. But it is necessary to remind ourselves that it is *people* who have objectives—the organization is only the mechanism necessarily established to ensure that objectives beyond the reach of an individual can be achieved through collective effort. To secure effectiveness and efficiency in attaining declared objectives, it is people who establish norms of behavior and performance for achievement through controlling arrangements under which rewards and resources are allocated or denied to individuals and groups. Thus rules, regulations, procedures, and conventions are introduced principally with the intention of controlling or facilitating behaviors of organizational members. These institutional requirements create the context and culture of the organization in which specialist roles and other functions are defined and partitioned, and relative positional status and responsibilities are identified. It is individuals and groups who are invested with authority to ensure that objectives are achieved through the coordination of collective effort.

Increasingly teachers are required to develop new skills to secure effective collaboration involved in working together on a regular basis, in the taking of collective decisions, and in group implementation of policies adopted. For most teachers, working in teams has—or will—become a permanent and continuous reality. Thus it is essential that the requirement for interdependent teamwork is recognized, acknowledged, and accepted as part of the requirements, responsibilities, and obligations of individual members in the development of effective groups.

Categories of followers: A tentative research typology

The author's current action research study, sponsored by the Norham Centre for Leadership Studies (NCLS) at the University of Oxford (Williams, 1998) and supported by the award of a personal Research Fellowship from The Leverhulme Trust, is focused on identifying the main characteristics of leader-follower relationships among experienced teachers in a group of schools in the Oxford region. In this study, a major hypothesis is that school effectiveness is achieved through the existence of high-quality leader-follower relationships in schools able to demonstrate a clear sense of collective purpose. A further question is to establish reasons for the individual election by some teachers to follow others in developing collaborative school cultures. Early in the study, and as already mentioned, this question emerged as a significant one as it became evident that teachers generally distrusted headteachers who were usually described by respondents as "visionary" or "charismatic." Other evidence in the initial study revealed a range of important personal variables as influential in the acceptance of follower roles.

From the inception of the research, it became clear that the term *follower* was inappropriate and inadequate to reflect "roles of personal choice" among respondents—not least because the word carried an implication of subordinate role delegation that is not commonly found among teachers. Thus, the term *contributor* was adopted and is used as the preferred term throughout the reporting of the current research.

Typically, when asked about the significance of individual contribution to both curriculum management and pupil progress in schools, several teachers clearly perceived personal roles as "taking a lead" and resented being regarded as merely "good classroom teachers" even though they were satisfied with their effort and success in those roles. In some schools, there appeared to be little explicit recognition of the high quality of their work, and virtually no praise for demonstrable achievement unless directly linked with academic success of students. Regrettably, it appeared that praise was offered sparingly—with success being attributed to abilities of students rather than to teaching effort and skill. Virtually no one reported examples of praise being given for the organization or management of curricular or pastoral (counseling) activities.

Elective contributors: The preferred teacher perception

Data from the present research study clearly indicate that among teachers the meaning conveyed by *contributor* rather than *follower* represents a new perspective in the continuing evolution of a conceptualization of leadership. Certainly, it conveys a more complete perception of role requirements in functioning either as leaders or followers. An important preliminary focus has been on ways in which individuals make, or withhold, positive contributions to the organizational development of schools. For example, the ways in which individuals participate in organizational growth rather than tacitly accepting the lead from those holding more senior appointed status are essentially controlled by personal rather than objectively rational perceptions.

From the NCLS/Leverhulme Trust research study a tentative categorization of elective "contributors" has emerged (Williams, 1995):

- *Positive:* Intellectually independent, thoughtfully constructive, takes personal ownership of both concepts and activities, especially valued and trusted by leaders.
- *Adversarial:* Antipathetic, soured by experience based on earlier unpleasant personal and professional discourtesies, generally suspicious, uncooperative, and resistant to change.
- *Compliant:* Conformist, conscientious, places complete trust in decisions of senior colleagues, has total acceptance of received wisdom.
- *Minimalist:* Conventionally sheeplike; a passive spectator of the entire life and work of the school beyond personal interests, with no holistic understanding.
- *Self-serving:* Egocentric, systematically selfish, active in micropolitical life-games in school, identified by others as untrustworthy and manipulative.

Preliminary feedback of the research findings to schools indicate that through using these categories, a clearer and more coherent understanding of interpersonal relationships has become accessible to both leaders and followers. Although not yet definitive, the categorization has provided useful agendas in some schools for development of greater collaborative activity leading to modification of attitudes and behavior through planned school improvement and professional self-development initiatives.

For example, it is recognized that in an idealized school every elective follower would be a positive contributor. Adversarial contributors would have suspicions and doubts eradicated through open, sensitive personal interaction with leaders. In effect, recognition of their potential value as positive contributors would have a transformational effect. Compliant contributors would be encouraged to assume broader perspectives and develop roles as positive contributors in recognition that new complexities in school organization and many differentiated roles demand greater commitment and visibility from good but self-effacing compliant practitioners. The message for minimalists is clear: it is no longer acceptable to be passive spectators, divorced from the broad spectrum of interlocking realities of the school's daily life with its many academic and social responsibilities in and beyond classrooms. Further, it is improbable that within regimes of increasingly constrained financial and personnel resources, schools have the capacity to accept any teachers as passengers who contribute little to the broader life and work of the school. Finally, the expenditure of scarce resources and time in counteracting the debilitating effects of the negative, selfish, counterproductive, and manipulative strategies of self-serving teachers is becoming increasingly unacceptable to their colleagues.

Effective schools cannot exist without even more effective teachers, and every school should ensure that all teachers are provided with genuine opportunities and encouraged to develop as positive contributors. Typically, school improvement strategies are derived from value systems with explicit "people" emphases: genuinely caring attitudes toward all individuals (students and parents, teachers and support staff), consensual agreement on holistic academic and social goals, individual commitment to personal and professional growth, and collective sensitivity to community expectations of high ethical standards.

The current research project suggests that traditional attitudes, which have led to confused messages about leadership in schools, should now be set aside. Inevitably, managers have subordinates whereas leaders cannot exist without elective followers. Because of the unique professional culture of education, positional leaders should seek to nurture teachers as essential contributors in the formulation and achievement of collective goals of schools. Former management traditions, mainly drawn from industrial and commercial models, often caricatured classroom practitioners as submissive, powerless, and unthinking followers. These notions are being gradually replaced by views of classroom practitioners as active, collaborative contributors in the undertaking of holistic organizational tasks, who should not be limited exclusively to classroom teaching roles. Indeed, a conclusion drawn from the research data is that as teachers are expensive educational resources (although grossly underremunerated in the United Kingdom) they should be encouraged to become positive contributors in the development of holistic school cultures.

In the further development of leadership theory and practice in all professional organizations, it will be necessary to accept that concepts of leading and following are essentially interdependent and complementary. They are neither competitive nor submissive roles but are interchangeable—typically found in exemplary work groups and task teams in all types of organizations.

As indicated earlier, initial reaction to the current NCLS/ Leverhulme Trust study has been favorable in that it provides a new balance between polarities of positional and earned leadership status and has moved concepts away from the earlier skewed emphasis found, for example, in the traditional Weberian hierarchical model. Further, the more dynamic appreciation of the critically important role of contributors in ensuring effectively distributed leadership in increasingly complex school organizations has been welcomed in the schools participating in the empirical phase of the research. It also reflects views of teachers— expressed by teachers who perceive themselves as positive, constructivist contributors and who daily and naturally assume professional leadership positions in schools (Williams, 1995; Lambert and others, 1996). Through acceptance of these important and valid perspectives, schools are developing shared leadership cultures reflecting Sergiovanni's "density of leadership" concept (1992) and the "earned leadership among teaching staff" concept of Williams (1989). The significance of this perception entails a reconceptualization of the teacher's role at initial and postexperience levels in organizational cultures that pursue school improvement strategies.

Conclusion

Current research indicates that the role of school management in a positional status framework in which distributed leadership roles are organizationally subsumed is gradually shifting its focus to become a consciously facilitating rather than a controlling mechanism. If professional leadership is to be effectively offered and applied in schools, the intentional development of roles on a shared, collective basis will require management skills of the highest order to create learning organizations. Earned leadership in learning organizations will entail stewardship of the value system, exploring and setting directions for new organizational design to facilitate personal and professional growth of all who contribute to improvement in educational provision for students. This research study indicates that increased effectiveness is visible in those schools already using earned leadership strategies. The data also reveal that teacher expectations for enduring and effective contributor roles rely explicitly on the development of earned leadership cultures coupled with a clear sense of personal worth through recognition as accomplished professionals in the pursuit of clear, agreed educational goals and associated tasks undertaken in schools.

In addition, fundamentally different relationships are required within a *professional leader–contributory follower* school culture than are evident in the controlling attitudes invariably found in differentiated manager-subordinate status relationships. For professional leaders there is a clear acknowledgment of an umbilical partnership with followers who elect to undertake, or accept, flexible roles in *contributing* to success in the life and work of schools. A characteristic example of sensitive responsiveness by school leaders may be seen through a shared understanding of when to provide school-wide leadership and when to follow colleagues who might expect to lead in technical or other specialties through teaching expertise and (or through) the exercise of personal choice.

Further exploration of the professional earned leader and elective contributor-follower relationship through a specifically sharper focus on followership concepts is the current thrust of the NCLS/Leverhulme Trust research. The interim perspective emerging from this study is that as educators experiencing both leader and follower roles we need to recognize, learn, and celebrate a new understanding that *following* is in dynamic relationship with *leading*. That both roles are interdependent, complementary, and elective is indisputable and should become a reality embedded in school cultures. The central task of school leaders now and into the early years of the next millennium, aware that school organization will be modified in a variety of unprecedented ways, is the creation of professional culture in anticipation of a time when schools may be held together only by their shared value systems.

References

Barth, R. S. *Improving Schools from Within: Teachers, Parents, and Principals Can Make the Difference.* San Francisco: Jossey-Bass, 1990.

Bennis, W., and Nanus, B. *Leaders: The Strategies for Taking Charge.* New York: HarperCollins, 1985.

Burns, J. M. *Leadership.* New York: HarperCollins, 1978.

Covey, S. R. *The Seven Habits of Highly Effective People.* New York: Simon & Schuster, 1990.

Drucker, P. *Management.* London: Pan Books, 1980.

Fullan, M. G. *The New Meaning of Educational Change.* London: Cassell, 1991.

Johnson, S. M. *Teachers at Work.* New York: Basic Books, 1990.

Kouzes, J. M., and Posner, B. Z. *The Leadership Challenge: How to Get Extraordinary Things Done in Organizations.* (Rev. ed.) San Francisco: Jossey-Bass, 1995.

Lambert, L., Collay, M., Dietz, M., Kent, K., and Richert, A. *Who Will Save Our Schools?* Thousand Oaks, Calif.: Corwin Press, 1996.

Lieberman, A. (ed.). *Building a Professional Culture in Schools.* New York: Teachers College Press, 1988.

Mintzberg, H. *The Structure of Organizations.* New York: Wiley, 1979.

Peters, T. J., and Waterman, R. H. *In Search of Excellence.* New York: HarperCollins, 1982.

Senge, P. *The Fifth Discipline.* New York: Doubleday, 1990.

Sergiovanni, T. J. *Moral Leadership: Getting to the Heart of School Improvement.* San Francisco: Jossey-Bass, 1992.

Weick, K. E. "Managerial Thought in the Context of Action." In S. Srivasta and Associates, *The Executive Mind: New Insights on Managerial Thought and Action.* San Francisco: Jossey-Bass, 1983.

White, R. P., Hodgson, P., and Crainer, S. *The Future of Leadership.* London: Pitman, 1996.

Williams, V. "Schools and Their Communities: Issues in External Relations." In J. Sayer and V. Williams (eds.), *Schools and External Relations: Managing the New Partnerships.* London: Cassell, 1989.

Williams, V. (ed.). *Towards Self-Managing Schools.* London: Cassell, 1995.

Williams, V. (ed.). *Making Learning Communities Work: The Critical Role of Leader as Learner.* New Directions for School Leadership, no. 7. San Francisco: Jossey-Bass, 1998.

VIVIAN WILLIAMS *is fellow in education, St. Peter's College, University of Oxford, director of the Norham Centre for Leadership Studies, and a research fellow of The Leverhulme Trust.*

*After five years as headteacher of a secondary school,
the author reflects on the daily realities of policy and
practice in developing a collaborative leadership
culture among colleagues during a period of cultural
change at school and community levels.*

2

Looking back from the front:
Practical reflections on leadership

David Johnson

IN ENGLAND AND WALES the quest to become a headteacher
(school principal) is a professional and emotional roller-coaster
ride. For the applicant there are aspirations, fears, confidence, and
doubt in approximately equal proportions. The writing of applications and preparation for interviews are stimulating processes but
time-consuming. If invited, the two or even three days of interview
can prove to be a juggling act of nerve, skill, knowledge, and inspi-
ration.

The key ability is to make the interviewing panel hear what they
wish to hear in addition to those messages you wish to communicate to them. Among many conceptual areas for a candidate to
explore fully is that of leading the school to higher levels of
achievement and success. How does a potential headteacher con-
vince an interviewing panel of his or her leadership skills and abilities? Once appointed, how does the successful candidate turn
promise and theory into effective action? Simple questions to

NEW DIRECTIONS FOR SCHOOL LEADERSHIP, NO. 9, FALL 1998 © JOSSEY-BASS PUBLISHERS

frame—but reflections on almost five years of headship in a 1000-student secondary (high) school reveal the enormous difficulty of attempting to find easy answers.

Initial leadership moves

In England and Wales, it is rare to have the luxury of time to consider accepting a senior appointment. Successful candidates are offered the post immediately following completion of interviews, often by an exhausted and relieved panel of school governors, and an instant decision has to be made. Frequently, candidates are prepared to move to a new geographical area to secure a headship, yet knowledge of the school can be limited to what has been learned from documentation and during the interview process. The leadership style of one's predecessor may remain shrouded in some mystery, to be gleaned and clarified through informal discussion or questioning. A key element in being interviewed successfully is often either to offer a completely new approach to leading the school or to promise to extend the style and sustain the values of the outgoing headteacher. Yet to offer more of the same might be perceived as an indication of weak or nonexistent leadership skills.

In my own situation it was clear that changes were overdue. The qualities of my retiring predecessor were many but there was little evidence of a hands-on approach to the day-to-day business of the school, which was performing reasonably well but had the potential for considerable development. In retrospect it seems simplistic that my emphasis on the headteacher being approachable (open door policy in the extreme), being out and about the school campus (comfortably the easiest of all duties and yet the most public display of "leadership"), and making ready verbal contact with staff and students were crucial elements in moving the school forward. A more collaborative style of leadership was overdue, a basic philosophy highlighted by Hargreaves (1992): "Collegiality is rapidly becoming one of the new orthodoxies of educational change and school improvement. Advocates of collegiality have shown little modesty in proclaiming its virtue" (p. 80).

However, improved verbal and written communications within and beyond the school (weekly newsletters, regular briefing papers, a formal structure to ensure the exchange and circulation of the minutes of all meetings), and active participation or support of staff and students both during and outside lesson times have proved to be essential ingredients in creating a team ethos and leading the school toward greater levels of achievement. There is, of course, reluctance in some quarters and criticism in others. Among the most important leadership skills involve purposeful questioning of the reluctance of some staff to see themselves as part of a team and to respond to suggestions or criticism of decisions both positively and professionally. Changing one's mind in the light of an alternative view, cogently argued and properly analyzed, may be difficult—but on a few occasions has proved to be a major positive quality in the eyes of some colleagues. Changing one's view simply to appease critical comment would rightly be seen as a weakness. Standing up to the critic or cynic whose comment or argument has little depth and is not in the school's best interest is, in my view, a substantial part of being a strong leader in school. It has also proved to be a fascinating part of my work.

Leadership through collaborative activity

I believe it is crucial to see the school as a series of "interlocking and mutually supportive teams, each the subject of well directed leadership" (Spence, 1993, p. 24). But to reach high levels of consistent, mutual support it is necessary to "go through the pain barrier" of challenge, focused discussion, and professional argument. Teamwork and the sharing of philosophy and values across curriculum divisions are keys to whole-school success. More than twenty years ago, members of Her Majesty's Inspectorate noted (Department of Education and Science, 1977) that the thread of consistency in successful schools was positive leadership: "What they [successful schools] all have in common is effective leadership and a 'climate' that is conducive to growth. . . . The foundation of their work and corporate life is an acceptance of shared values. Emphasis is laid on consultation, team work and participation, but without exception, the most important single factor is the quality of leadership of the head" (p. 36).

In any school, the empowerment of all staff to participate in the decision-making process is a key precursor of development, innovation, and ultimately success in its widest form. The major difficulty lies in empowering those colleagues who do not recognize the need or do not wish to be thus empowered. The defeatist syndrome—"senior staff are paid to make the decisions, so let them get on with it"—which all too often is a feature of staff lounges must be challenged in a manner that is both encouraging and convincing to colleagues who display such naïveté on one hand and such cynicism on the other. In my own situation, the establishment of a clear meeting schedule in which one meeting informs the next in a logical sequence, the creation of open-access staff working groups tasked to address a wide range of issues, and the opening up of the deliberations of the senior leadership team (which now includes an additional member, drawn from staff volunteers on an annual basis) have had a considerable impact on the "knowledge base" of the school.

During a consultancy project in a school, Reynolds and Cuttance (1992) identified a familiar need to demystify the workings of the senior management team, making public its discussions and decision-making processes. Strategies were employed to "solidify the staff group and make it reform around a new body of knowledge that [had been] interpreted as good practice . . . encouraging the staff to 'take on' their management" (p. 181).

There have, of course, been failures. Not all staff working groups produced positive results; there is still uncertainty in some quarters, and some colleagues' involvement is minimal. However, there is clear evidence of change in the culture of the school and as new staff are appointed, further progress is being made. I see my own role as the presenter of a clear example to colleagues (and students) that enthusiastically promotes collective involvement in the school's activities and decision-making processes.

At a simple micro-level, school events become our (collective) events to be supported by as many staff as possible (within the natural constraints of family and out-of-school life). At a macro-level I agree with Bennis and Nanus (1985) that we should all see ourselves as "movers and shakers" in the school's best interests: "catalysts . . . [committed] to a common enterprise . . . and capable of sustaining a vision that encompasses the whole organization" (p. 216).

This may be summed up simply as leading from the front and, crucially, as sweeping others up in the wake. This approach to leadership activity and philosophy, labeled "transformative leadership" by Bennis and Nanus (1985), has significant strength: "It is collective, there is a symbiotic relationship between leaders and followers, and what makes it collective is the subtle interplay between the followers' needs and wants and the leader's capacity to understand, one way or another, these collective aspirations" (p. 217).

Critically, the end result of development and empowerment of colleagues rather than the more prosaic, functional management of coworkers is a school more likely to embrace change positively, either self-generated or externally imposed, and to work successfully as a cohesive whole for the benefit of its students. The maxim often brought to mind is again provided by Bennis and Nanus (1985): "Leadership stands in the same relationship to empowerment that management does to compliance" (p. 218).

Team leadership and progressive development

Leadership is a collaborative activity. The headteacher cannot plough a lone furrow at the head of the school. There are always key players within the staff team to whom tasks and responsibilities are delegated and who are both followers and yet leaders in their own right. This cascading of leadership spawns new leaders throughout the school. Handy (1993) believes the task of a leader is "to develop and communicate a vision which gives meaning to the work of others" (p. 117), a perception defined and amplified somewhat earlier by Williams (1989): "Leaders cannot exist without followers. . . . In its essentials, leadership is the power to influence the thinking and behaviour of others to achieve mutually desired objectives" (p. 24).

Targeting the key positive colleagues was a major initial task following my appointment to the headship of the school. Similarly, the targeting of key negative players was an early priority in order to plan strategies that, over time, would lead to changes in behaviors and attitudes. The latter exercise is far more testing than the former. However, key players cannot be identified by status alone. During initial contacts with colleagues there is, for any newly appointed headteacher, a careful balancing act of meeting, listening (to attitudes as well as levels of knowledge), observing (on and off task), and evaluating abstractions such as commitment and willingness to embrace change—all the while paying special attention to the need to become aware of specific personal ambition of individuals prior to identifying key leaders within the staff group.

The tension between the need to identify strategic team players early in the process and to avoid making errors through hasty judgment was considerable. However, the planning and execution by a team of staff of a Saturday conference, attended after some persuasive argument by around 90 percent of the teachers (plus some members of the school's governing board and nonteaching staff of the school) revealed most judgments to be correct. Similarly, a clear policy of bringing the whole staff together, at least for part of professional development days held five times during each school year, at a staff forum organized half-termly, and for a weekly Friday morning ten-minute briefing session, has proved effective in terms of high-visibility leadership and also to promote team building throughout the school. Establishing the pattern of events was relatively simple; ensuring that the content of each meeting is relevant and stimulating has kept the adrenaline flowing. The scheduling of a second conference within a few months was, perhaps, a successful performance indicator.

Encouraging and convincing colleagues to become mainstream players in the school's activities and development demands high levels of application and personal enthusiasm. The quest for clear distributed leadership has remained undimmed but has, naturally, taken sideways steps on occasion. Without doubt, the most difficult aspect of being the leader of the school has been cultivating the kind of leadership that Adams (1987) describes as being "prepared to share and delegate responsibility and promote real participation in discussion and decision-making . . . the ability to motivate, direct and evaluate" (p. 154). There are days when I think I am close to this nirvana, but there are other days . . . !

An inclusive culture

The enabling of colleagues to participate more fully in the development of the school—that is, making them feel comfortable and confident to do so—has proved to be an important application of personal leadership style and skills. Many, though by no means all, teachers or members of the nonteaching staff have been liberated from former reactive roles and now play a full, proactive part in the school's daily life or in strategic forward planning. The concept of "the staff as a whole" rather than "teachers and others" has been a major thrust; any hint of subjugation or elitism within the staffing establishment is challenged forcefully.

In many schools there is still a feeling of "them and us"—for example, between senior and other staff, or between teachers and those who work in administration or as technicians, site supervisors, and in similar occupations. My view is that the wise headteacher, as the leading professional in the school, will include all members of the staffing establishment equally, however difficult the process may be or however reluctant or uncertain some colleagues may appear.

After five years I still see much to be done in this respect. However, the philosophy is well articulated and is now echoed, almost subconsciously, by key players in the school. Significantly, those previously in "less important" positions feel more comfortable if it is necessary to challenge their erstwhile "superiors." In this sense, perhaps all headteachers would be wise to pay due attention to the reported experience of Peters and Waterman (1982): "What we found was that associated with almost every excellent company was a strong leader (or two) who seemed to have had a lot to do with making the company excellent in the first place" (p. 26).

The leading professional

Leading any school is a multifaceted concept. There are many audiences looking to the headteacher for guidance and example. The staff of the school await with some expectation as the new-comer takes up the post. In the United Kingdom the school governors, whose judgment has been tested in the initial appointment process, also wait and observe as their collective decision is personified. The Local Education Authority, now with significantly reduced influence over most schools, casts a professional eye on the development of the school. Crucially, parents and the students also seek to analyze the strengths and weaknesses of the new head-teacher. Being an effective leader in so many different contexts proved to be one of the most demanding aspects of my early months in post. It continues to be so!

If prompted to identify major pieces in the leadership jigsaw puzzle, I should point to high visibility in school and the local community, a willingness to speak out—and sometimes fight—for the school's best interests against local or national politics or policies, and an overwhelmingly enthusiastic willingness to work with school governors for the school's benefit. Nevertheless, this last-named duty of being the school's leading professional is sometimes a considerably frustrating one. Meetings of the governing board of the school are usually scheduled during evenings after a full day's work, and involve working with governors possessing hugely differing levels of understanding of educational and other issues. However, through discussion, explanation, and occasional bouts of heated debate, a mutual regard has developed. The sixteen people in this disparate group, powerful enough to make massive decisions affecting both the daily life of the school and also its future direction, are now sufficiently focused and informed to feel comfortable in their deliberations.

My own sense of circumspection as the school's leader in this different context tells me that even now, I should never take any matter for granted; governors' meetings are invariably hard work in the most positive sense. My two deputy headteacher colleagues (assistant principals) who also attend governors' meetings as observers, are equally alert, should our collective concentration and attention to detail wane. As leaders themselves, they are quick to add relevant facts or provide explanatory details, and a rather unsophisticated system of body language and para-linguistics helps us keep pace with debate at governors' meetings. I regard my deputies' attendance at meetings as essential.

The school and its community

During the school day it has proved invaluable to invite governors to participate in lessons, school events, or activities. Such involvement is part of our team building and the sharing of knowledge about how the school actually feels on a day-to-day basis. Sharing knowledge and experiences naturally involves the development of shared values—which, according to Peters and Waterman (1982, p. 240) lie at the heart of the most successful enterprises. "People orientation . . . high expectations and peer review" have become mutual expectations not only within the governing body but also between school-based staff and school governors, of which the headteacher is one. A governors' self-audit of strengths and weaknesses in relation to educational issues and school governance—and the development of a subsequent action plan to address shortfalls—is currently proving to be an important element in bonding together members of this non–school-based team.

For students and many parents, the headteacher is a figure of authority, either simply as a result of his or her status or perhaps because of an ingrained, traditional view of school hierarchies. I am doubtful if *figure of authority* and *leader* are necessarily inter-changeable terms, nor is status necessarily linked directly with respect. Colleagues who seek refuge in (or self-defense through) positional status rather than trust and reliance in earned status would rightly be regarded with suspicion. However, in the devel-oping mind of the student body there is nevertheless a naturally immature dimension that assists in the judgment of the head-teacher's qualities. Students certainly look toward their headteacher as the positional leader of the school and in an early initiative I endeavored to include students in the school's decision-making processes. Student councils had never previously existed and their establishment promised an important new aspect to relationships among all members of the school community. Initially, pastoral leaders among the staff enthusiastically embraced the idea of reg-ular meetings with representative groups of students, but the framework and direction were not sufficiently well established.

Despite some fertile periods, the various student councils even-tually fell into disarray. Too much direct leading by the headteacher or not enough? Such failure serves as instruction and we are now planning how to establish more successful and longer-term coun-cils at which the student voice and opinion may be genuinely heard. Attempts to work successfully with students, to encourage parents to become members of monitoring groups, or to bring all staff and governors into the front line of whole-school discussion are encap-sulated by Fullan's assertion (1992) that the headteacher's main task is not found in "implementing innovations or even in instructional leadership for specific classrooms. The larger task is in transform-ing the culture of the school. . . . The Principal as the collaborative leader is the key to this future" (p. 13).

School leadership means leading within and beyond the school. On a day-to-day or strategic planning level it is relatively easy to be a high-profile "chair" or contributor to the round of meetings that typifies all schools. The assigned scope of the various groups meeting at school has widened considerably following the welcome arrival of site-based management organization. During my first year in the post, it was clear that there was an expectation that the new headteacher would chair almost every meeting at which whole-school issues were debated. In the short term this was an effective device for mutual evaluation and familiarization.

There was, however, a feeling that a greater sharing of the tasks associated with being the convener of a meeting—agenda preparation, negotiation with colleagues about the timing of specific topics for discussion, chairing the subsequent meeting, ensuring effective minuting and dissemination of information—would broaden the leadership principle among the staff. At the end of a self-imposed twelve-month acceptance of being chair to all groups, I successfully delegated the task to a range of colleagues who consult and discuss widely, but who also accept their responsibilities for getting the show on the road.

Leadership beyond the school, at various local groups and in national and international contexts, is clearly a major responsibility of the headteacher, but one that can be shared with other colleagues. I firmly believe that active membership of working parties or advisory groups at county or national levels and participation in significant, relevant conferences are important vehicles for making known the school's strengths, successes, and general good educational practice.

There is, of course, a tension. An absent leader is not a good leader and participation in out-of-school events has to be monitored carefully—a relatively easy matter. More difficult is to challenge the perception of some colleagues that personal promotion may precede promotion of the school as a center of excellence. However, providing colleagues with opportunities to explore the wider issues and simultaneously raise the school's profile can be an effective leadership device. For example, enabling colleagues to train as school inspectors and participate in one or two inspections each year increases awareness of their own school's strengths and weaknesses, and allows them to gain recognition for the school and for themselves elsewhere. Similarly, inviting the deputy headteachers to represent the school at significant conferences or meetings and encouraging other colleagues to contribute to international conferences or teacher exchanges have all resulted in the school's name and reputation extending beyond the previously parochial circle in which it operated.

More simply, the appointment of a press officer from within the school's existing staff ensures that we have regular, high-quality coverage in the local media. In simple economic terms, the better known the school and the stronger its reputation, the more it will be chosen by parents for their children. Excellence within the school—for example, through good national examination results, effective disciplinary records, and a deserved reputation for sensitive pastoral care—can be matched and enhanced by the school's name being naturally and positively associated with initiatives or organizations in the wider community.

Conclusion

The quality of a school's staff is one of its most important attributes. It seems appropriate within the scope of this contribution to conclude with reference to several key actions and beliefs that have been interpreted as strong, determined leadership. First, a personal readiness to take issue both with underperforming teachers and also with members of the nonteaching staff. Second, an alacrity in challenging cynicism and negative influences in the school. Third, a determination to recruit, retain, and develop high-quality staff who are committed to the task in hand.

There have been some remarkable successes. Equally, there is still some distance to travel and there have been disappointments. However, the collective policy and philosophy are now clearly mapped. New colleagues joining the school know that there are clear expectations. Our appointment procedures and documentation have been completely refashioned in a new house style to signal our determination that only our collaborative best will do. We owe that to our students.

On looking back from the front, a personally appropriate conclusion from Peters and Waterman (1982) might be offered to leading practitioners: "The specific content of the dominant beliefs of the excellent companies is . . . narrow in scope, including just a few basic values. A belief in being the best. . . . A belief in the importance of people as individuals. . . . A belief that most members of the organization should be innovators, and its corollary, the willingness to support failure" (p. 283).

References

Adams, N. *Secondary School Management Today.* London: Hutchinson, 1987.

Bennis, W., and Nanus, B. *Leaders: The Strategies for Taking Charge.* New York: HarperCollins, 1985.

Department for Education and Science. *Ten Good Schools: A Secondary School Enquiry.* London: Her Majesty's Stationery Office, 1977.

Fullan, M. G. *Successful School Improvement.* Buckingham, England: Open University Press, 1992.

Handy, C. *Understanding Organizations.* Harmondsworth, England: Penguin, 1993.

Hargreaves, A. "Contrived Collegiality: The Micropolitics of Teacher Collaboration." In N. Bennett, M. Crawford, and C. Riches (eds.), *Managing Change in Education.* London: Chapman, 1992.

Peters, T. J., and Waterman, R. H. *In Search of Excellence.* New York: HarperCollins, 1982.

Reynolds, D., and Cuttance, P. *School Effectiveness.* London: Cassell, 1992.

Spence, B. "What's in a Team?" In "Secondary School Management in the 1990s: Challenge and Change." *Journal of the Institute of Education, University of Hull*, 1993, *48*, 24.

Williams, V. "Schools and Their Communities: Issues in External Relations." In J. Sayer and V. Williams (eds.), *Schools and External Relations: Managing the New Partnerships.* London: Cassell, 1989.

DAVID JOHNSON *is headteacher of William Parker School, Daventry, Northamptonshire, United Kingdom.*

The authors provide an account of a public-private partnership designed to improve elementary science education by employing principles of collaborative leadership to involve all major stakeholders.

3

Collaborative leadership and partnership management

William J. Casile, Reeny D. Davison

IN THE UNITED STATES, the one-room schoolhouse is a historical icon, a model for the preparation and acculturation of future generations. This singularly committed organization was the locus of every community's hope for its children, the place where parents sent their children to "get an education" and be prepared to respond to the demands of an evolving democratic social context. Children were not just sent to the school, they were entrusted to it. As parents were distracted by the daily tasks necessary to ensure the survival of their families and their communities, they trusted that the school was about its important chore of equipping their children with the knowledge, skills, and attitudes needed to ensure their ability to survive and perhaps thrive in the sometimes uncertain climate of the evolving near future.

Parents' hope for the success of their children and the communities' trust in their future survival was dependent on the teaching and learning that occurred within the four walls of the schoolhouse. These educational processes were under the direct supervision of

NEW DIRECTIONS FOR SCHOOL LEADERSHIP, NO. 9, FALL 1998 © JOSSEY-BASS PUBLISHERS

the solitary figure in charge of this sacred trust, the schoolteacher. Albeit a person usually hired by a representative committee from the community, the teacher was typically left unfettered to be the educational leader and the manager of the school. The teacher was uniquely responsible for the design and delivery of the full content of the curriculum and the eventual success of the students. Certainly the family and the church were other significant institutional forces in the development of children, but the schoolhouse's force in this developmental process was equally fundamental.

As American culture very quickly moved from a survival focus to a success focus for large numbers of citizens, community and parental hopes for children rose. It was no longer enough for schools to prepare children so that they could just persevere, it was expected that schools would prepare children to thrive, to move beyond past generations—to shape the future, not just survive it. This cultural generativity or concern for providing the next generation with a better "quality of life" remains the hallmark and the promise of education.

Throughout the last century, public schools in America emerged from and promoted the general goals of a democratic society: to improve social conditions, to promote cultural unity, to foster economic self-sufficiency, to prepare responsible citizens, and to enrich the lives of individuals (Dewey, [1900] 1990, 1916; Center on National Education Policy, 1996). From the beginning, these public institutions have been the setting for broad social debate over the central purpose of education. Attempts to reconcile the apparent dilemmas of schools charged with enabling individuals to achieve economic prosperity and "pursue happiness," and to promote the broader social need for all to support the "common good" and a civil society, have changed little during our nation's life span (Apple and Beane, 1995).

The evolution of education in this country, and elsewhere in the world, has been the product of significant changes in socioeconomic and cultural pressures (Williams, 1995) and the continuing desire to promote democratic schools in support of the "commonwealth" (Darling-Hammond, 1996). The educational system has evolved from an era of independent one-room schools to schools operating within increasingly complex and interdependent social, cultural, and economic systems. However, the community's expectation of the school as the vehicle for individual as well as cultural enhancement remains constant. The mission of education must continue to emphasize equitable opportunities for achievement. What has changed, and must continue to evolve, are the ways in which schools must operate and cooperate to fulfill this mission effectively.

Today, no school is able to operate in isolation. Similarly, no educational leader can be successful operating in the isolation offered by bureaucratic authority (Sergiovanni and Starratt, 1998). There are two forces that militate against a return to the simplicity and unitary control structure modeled by the one-room schoolhouse and replicated in larger, hierarchical school systems. First, the functional demands placed on the school have increased significantly as we race into a future that becomes obsolete at an increasingly faster rate. Second, bureaucratic leadership does not support the most basic mission of education in a democratic society, that is, to provide opportunities to learn for all students. To augment the organizational capacity needed to promote world-class achievement for all students, schools must seek partnerships with external agents and agencies seeking to support improved school outcomes. The primary agents claiming stakeholder status include federal, state, and local governments and agencies; universities; professional organizations and unions; foundations and the corporate community; and parents (Newman and Wehlage, 1995). These stakeholders, some demanding to be included in shaping the form of schools and others waiting to be invited, are not well accommodated by hierarchical leadership structures.

Speaking to the issue of leadership efficacy, Sergiovanni and Starratt (1998) do not dispute the legitimacy of the bureaucratic source of authority; they instead emphasize that the consequences of supervision and leadership models based on hierarchy, rules and regulations, mandates, and role prescriptions are not consistent with the tenets of a democratic and professional community. "Without proper monitoring, teachers wind up being loosely connected to bureaucratic systems, complying only when they have to. When monitoring is effective in enforcing compliance, teachers respond as technicians who execute predetermined scripts and whose performance is narrow" (p. 39). In either event, teachers, who need to be primary professional leaders, are relegated to the periphery of the educational enterprise.

To survive and to be effective promoting equitable opportunities for exemplary achievement, educational institutions must be willing to abandon ties to bureaucratic authority and cultivate collaborative leaders, partners, and followers. The next section offers an example of a broad-based, comprehensive science education program that seeks to enhance instructional delivery systems through the generation and nurturance of collaborative leadership.

Collaborative leadership: The ASSET example

Established in 1993, ASSET (Allegheny Schools Science Education and Technology) Inc. is an independent nonprofit organization dedicated to improving the science and technology achievement of all students in the city of Pittsburgh and Allegheny County, Pennsylvania. The organization, made up of a board of directors, officers, and staff, comprises a network of partners from business and industry, public education, higher education, and agencies representing various science-related resources in the region. The inaugural partners included the Bayer Corporation, Allegheny Intermediate Unit (a state-funded educational service agency), Carnegie Science Center, Duquesne University, the Learning Research and Development Center of the University of Pittsburgh, and participating school districts within Allegheny County. Each partner contributes expertise and resources representative of its capabilities and interests. For example, fundraising and public relations expertise is provided by Bayer, expertise in science education and leadership by Duquesne University, and program evaluation by the Learning Research and Development Center.

The organization promotes and supports implementation by school districts of a comprehensive elementary science program. This program includes the selection of nationally validated science curriculum materials, a centralized material supply and support center, a system of professional development opportunities, community involvement strategies, and the development of appropriate performance assessments and program evaluation methods (Loucks-Horsley and others, 1990).

Program implementation is funded by fees from participating schools, by grants from various corporate and private foundations, and by a five-year, multimillion-dollar National Science Foundation (NSF) grant (National Science Foundation, 1994). Currently, ASSET directly supports inquiry-based science instruction for 25,000 students and 1,020 teachers in the sixty-three elementary schools of sixteen school districts in Allegheny County. The program is committed to building direct support for all forty-three school districts within the county and providing technical assistance to others interested in replicating the program design.

ASSET and the context of elementary science education

Essential to an understanding of what ASSET has been able to accomplish is an examination of how ASSET has chosen to organize and operate in relationship to the existing contextual system of public education in this region. Allegheny County, with the Pittsburgh Public Schools as its large urban core surrounded by forty-two independent suburban districts, presents a unique school district environment. The county's school districts differ considerably in enrollment and in organizational culture. Enrollment in the smallest suburban school district is barely over one thousand students while the Pittsburgh Public Schools serve over forty thousand students. The racial profiles and socioeconomic demographics of these schools represent similar ranges of disparity while reflecting the range of diversity found in this region. Since each district is an autonomous and independent authority, it typically operates in isolation, designing and implementing curriculum within broad guidelines provided by the Pennsylvania Department of Education. Thus each participating district has developed a scope and sequence for the delivery of its elementary science curriculum. To manage this range of diversity, ASSET operates with a collaborative leadership and partner management style that requires all partners to maintain a tight focus on the vision—continuous improvement of science education for all children—while fostering diverse and individualized implementation strategies needed to ensure success in sixteen districts with unique organizational and community cultures.

The primary collaborative structure established to simultaneously allow districts to meet their unique needs and begin to foster interdistrict cooperation is the Coalition Leadership Teams. These teams of teachers and administrators from all districts in a particular coalition reflect ASSET's requirement that individual districts must form collaborative partnerships with other districts to coordinate their use of materials and to plan professional development activities. From this basic structure, a myriad of roles to promote interdistrict communication and coordination (essential to the change process) were established (Hurd, Rutherford, Huling-Austin, and Hall, 1987). Functional role descriptions for Building Lead Teachers (the building-level expert consultants and trainers) and the Support On Site team members (the districts' principal liaisons with ASSET) have evolved into formal collaborative elements. However, having these and other collaborative structures in place does not guarantee a collaborative culture in which cross-district support and interactions are the norm. It is anticipated that as more districts become involved and committed to working together, they will experience the benefits provided by cross-district collaboration and they will embrace it and promote it more aggressively.

A second area of collaboration fostered by the emergence of the ASSET program is the unprecedented involvement of regional institutions interested in supporting the improvement of elementary science education. Allegheny County is replete with such organizations—it has a diverse and supportive business and philanthropic community, universities, and a host of regional science resource agencies. Over the past two years, many of these institutions have become partners in the ASSET program and aligned their resources to support its comprehensive, inquiry-based approach to teaching science. These organizations have capitalized on this unique opportunity to support the unified science curriculum framework supported by ASSET. Prior to ASSET, these organizations had to negotiate arrangements with forty-three separate and distinct school districts and approaches to science curricula. For example, local foundations can now maximize their investment in regional institutions and schools by referring petitioners with project proposals to enhance elementary science first to ASSET for alignment with its science curriculum framework before they fund new projects.

From the inclusive ASSET perspective, each of these institutions offers unique expertise and resources that can be marshaled to effect measurable movement toward the vision of exemplary science instruction promulgated by the National Science Foundation program evaluations. For example, recent recommendations resulting from data analysis of recent NSF-guided program evaluations indicate that elementary teachers working with ASSET need more explicit instruction in the science concepts and principles found in the units of instruction that make up the ASSET curriculum framework. Equipped with these data, ASSET is able to promote and support partnerships between elementary teachers and the regional science institutions best able to collaborate on this professional development challenge. However, these collaborative partnerships require more than just a commitment to a common cause. The interpersonal and intergroup dynamics that emerge when new relationships are formed and individuals and institutions struggle with issues of trust and responsibility must also be managed with a collaborative spirit if these partners are to realize their potential for unique contributions to the vision. The following sections explore the elements of collaborative leadership.

Elements of ASSET's collaborative leadership

The elements of collaborative leadership and partnership management essential to ASSET's success are validated in the literature of systemic change and organizational development supporting the process of successful school restructuring (Newman and Wehlage, 1995). In addition, the creation of these collaborative structures as a means to promote systemic reforms has been confirmed by the NSF competition for funding systemic change grants. In its grant solicitation and guidelines (1994), the NSF requires applicants to describe the collaborative structures and methods that will be used to promote fundamental changes in the ways that schools deliver science instruction. As a private, independent organization attempting to construct and sustain a network of partnerships among a diverse array of parties invested in science education, ASSET uses collaboration as an invitation to participate in the creation of a culture with norms of shared responsibility and decision making, open communications, trust, and mutual interdependence. The following are the elements of collaborative leadership and partnership management incorporated into and modeled by ASSET:

• *Developing and articulating the vision.* It is generally accepted that envisioning the future is an essential process for the success of any organization (Quigley, 1993; Kouzes and Posner, 1995). To be able to build consensus for what the ideal future should be is a primary task of collaborative leadership. In ASSET, the characteristics of the best approaches to elementary science education are continuously reviewed in an effort to promote clarity and seek consensus. Initially, this involves sending teams of participating teachers and administrators to a national leadership conference in elementary science education conducted by the National Science Resources Center (1997). This provides a foundation of understanding for the nature and elements of a comprehensive elementary science program. These teams, along with additional teachers and administrators from participating districts and scientists or consultants from other partnering organizations, are invited to participate in the annual ASSET leadership conferences. These events provide arenas where local school leaders are invited to construct and build consensus for a common vision. This process is continued by routinely involving a large number of participants in strategic and tactical planning dialogues where organizational norms are clarified and communicated, and coalition teams are encouraged to personalize the ASSET vision for their participating districts.

• *Forming dynamic teams.* It is not enough to communicate the organization's vision, the communication must grab the attention and the hearts of people who will be motivated to act in support of efforts to make the vision become a reality. Who are the "right" partners? Who is enthusiastic, motivated to change, committed to finding a better way to do business? ASSET looks to stakeholders first, and prime among all stakeholders are those closest to the learning event—students and parents, teachers and administrators. Among these key participants in the teaching and learning of science are individuals who are attracted to the vision and the opportunity to participate in the collaborative culture that ASSET promises. One participant described his readiness to be involved with ASSET by saying, "The ASSET boat is going in the right direction and I want to be on board." For ASSET, and any organization looking to enlist dynamic team members in a start-up endeavor, the task is to identify stakeholders who are not just interested in going along for the ride—they're also carrying their own oar and looking for the right boat to help row.

According to Pugach and Johnson (1995), people who work effectively in collaborative organizations share certain characteristics. They recognize the value-added and creative nature of solutions developed through collaboration. They enjoy the social process and intellectual stimulation and growth of collective problem solving, and they value the process of reflection as a means to avoid the habituation of their practice. These characteristics can be useful criteria to help identify people who will make dynamic team members.

In ASSET, these dynamic team members are the parents, administrators, teachers, or scientists who are already motivated to change and, most important, are ready to embrace new roles for themselves so as to actualize their belief in the vision. Parents become volunteers in the material support center, teachers become teacher-trainers, administrators become program support people for a coalition of districts, scientists become teachers, all become innovators and team leaders, and they do it in service of a new vision for elementary education. They have become part of the ASSET team—a self-empowered team that is not just a group of members, but a dynamic community of leaders with a common vision. This teamwork is the opposite of teacher isolation and it is this teamwork that gets results (Katzenbach and Smith, 1993).

It is the norm for ASSET to foster collaboration by creating leadership opportunities and new roles for people who are motivated to embrace the vision. This has been especially true for teachers in the ASSET program. ASSET requires that teachers step out of their frequently isolated positions in classrooms to network with teachers and administrators from the other ASSET school districts and participants from ASSET partner organizations. This process thrusts teachers into leadership roles on the numerous task teams formed to plan and implement various elements of the ASSET initiative.

• *Sustaining collaborative systems of support.* Systemic change, organizational reform, and restructuring of educational institutions requires sustained, systematic commitment and effort. To move toward the continuous improvement of science education for all students, a systemic approach to change must be developed. The comprehensive approach to effective science programs, including the essential elements of quality materials, materials support, professional development, assessment, and community support, is part of that system—but it is not sufficient. Building consensus for a shared vision and forging a team of leaders from divergent partners are also elements of the system, but they are still inadequate to effect lasting systemic change in education. Successful programs like ASSET recognize the need for people working collaboratively to customize systems in ways that best support *their* desired outcomes in *their* unique organizations. This freedom to implement structures and processes that fit the individual needs and idiosyncratic norms of existing organizational cultures is a potent invitation to participate. For example, school districts are motivated to join because they share an enthusiasm for the vision, are confident in the competence and integrity of ASSET, and have not been asked to yield their autonomy in matters of instructional design and curriculum development.

- *Maintaining collaborative leadership.* Management of systemic change in a culturally cohesive yet structurally diverse environment demands that ASSET be a credible organization. To be credible, ASSET must practice what it preaches—"walk the talk," in current business jargon. As Kouzes and Posner (1995) point out, an organization that desires a leading role must do what it says it will do to promote credible leadership. Collaborative leadership means communicating and implementing the consensus aspirations and collective aims of the group through means that respect the elements of collaboration.

The program leadership sees its function as creating program credibility and a concomitant trust in ASSET, reinforcing its invitation to participate in a collaborative journey to a shared vision for elementary science education. ASSET believes that the successful management of systemic change initiatives is dependent on joining with a community of indigenous leaders to co-construct their most effective path to the desired future. To accomplish this, ASSET endeavors to model a leadership process consistent with its collaborative nature, which it refers to as the "Scramble" (Interview with V. Valicenti of ASSET Inc., Pittsburgh, Pa., Aug. 14, 1996). This metaphor is derived from the scramble format used in many golf tournaments. Each member of a team of golfers takes a shot from the tee. All members proceed to the "best ball" and proceed to play their second shots from this most advantageous position. In addition, the teammates are able to discuss variables that might influence their next shot, such as club selection, wind direction and targeting. Perhaps most important, each member of the team has the opportunity to observe the others' performance, learn from previous trials, and incorporate this new learning into the next performance. The results are always better than those individual golfers achieve when playing competitively.

Within the emerging model of the ASSET initiative, there are three concentrically arranged layers or structures that must operate collaboratively if credibility is to be maintained. The inner core is the ASSET board and staff. This relatively small group is central to the initiation and coordination of structures and activities designed to implement all aspects of this comprehensive approach to science education. The second layer is the school and district level. This stratum represents the internal elements of the system designed to deliver science education to students. It is the operational level and the traditional locus of the learning event. The final layer involves partnerships between the internal or school-based elements and those elements historically external to the classroom, which come together to support improvements in the current models of elementary science education. Each level represents new and unique relationships among diverse individuals and organizations. Each level faces parallel challenges related to trust and ownership that threaten the maintenance of the collaborative spirit.

The primary message that ASSET strives to convey about its leadership and partnership management style is that collaboration is the key to better planning, decision making, and implementation along the way to the desired future. By consistently modeling a leadership style that demands the collaboration inherent in the scramble format, the ASSET staff has earned credibility and the trust of its participating members. This central core of the initiative has developed a collaborative culture. The district and partnership levels have adopted collaborative structures, a first step toward a more collaborative culture.

Conclusion

In the ASSET model of leadership and partnership management, collaboration cannot be mandated. People must come to it because they trust that it is the appropriate way to improve the operation of their organizations. They cannot be forced to seek change, they must desire it. Collaborative leadership is an effective way to manage partnerships because it invites people to join in an adventure and to continue making additional choices about the tasks to be accomplished and about their commitment to the partnership (Kouzes and Posner, 1995). This genuine offer of choice is a process that builds trust and encourages ownership and responsibility from all participants who accept the invitation. It is this building of commitment that sustains investment and ensures goal accomplishment. The highly visible accomplishments achieved through participation in the ASSET network have created the energy that sustains the system. ASSET has gotten consensus on and support for building a better mousetrap, but people are rushing to become involved because of ASSET's invitation to them to set the trap in ways that will be most effective in their own organizations. In this collaborative culture, there is equal attention paid to getting the job done right and developing collaborative partnerships that will sustain the effort. Both competence and relationship building are important ASSET values.

References

Apple, M. W., and Beane, J. A. (eds.). *Democratic Schools*. Alexandria, Va.: Association for Supervision and Curriculum Development, 1995.

Center on National Education Policy. *Do We Still Need Public Schools?* Bloomington, Ind.: Phi Delta Kappa, 1996.

Darling-Hammond, L. "The Right to Learn and the Advancement of Teaching: Research, Policy, and Practice for Democratic Education." *Educational Researcher*, 1996, *25* (6), 5–17.

Dewey, J. *The School and Society*. Chicago: University of Chicago Press, 1990. (Originally published 1900.)

Dewey, J. *Democracy and Education*. New York: Macmillan, 1916.

Hurd, S. M., Rutherford, W. L., Huling-Austin, L., and Hall, G. E. *Taking Charge of Change*. Alexandria, Va.: Association for Supervision and Curriculum Development, 1987.

Katzenbach, J. R., and Smith, D. K. *The Wisdom of Teams*. New York: Harper-Business, 1993.

Kouzes, J. M., and Posner, B. Z. *The Leadership Challenge: How to Get Extraordinary Things Done in Organizations*. (Rev. ed.) San Francisco: Jossey-Bass, 1995.

Loucks-Horsley, S., Kapitan, R., Carlson, M., Kuberbis, P., Clark, R., Melle, G., Sachase, T., and Walton, E. *Elementary School Science for the 90s*. Alexandria, Va.: Association for Supervision and Curriculum Development, 1990.

National Science Foundation, Directorate for Education and Human Resources. "Local Systemic Change Through Teacher Enhancement,

Grades K–8, Solicitation and Guidelines." Arlington, Va.: National Science Foundation, 1994.

National Science Resources Center. "Science Education Leadership Institute." Washington, D.C.: National Science Resources Center, 1997.

Newman, F. M., and Wehlage, G. G. *Successful School Restructuring: A Report to the Public and Educators*. Madison, Wisc.: Center on Organization and Restructuring of Schools, 1995.

Pugach, M. C., and Johnson, L. J. *Collaborative Practitioners, Collaborative Schools*. Denver, Colo.: Love, 1995.

Quigley, J. V. *Vision: How Leaders Develop It, Share It, and Sustain It*. New York: McGraw-Hill, 1993.

Sergiovanni, T. J., and Starratt, R. J. *Supervision: A Redefinition*. (6th ed.). New York: McGraw-Hill, 1998.

Williams, V. "The Context of Development." In V. Williams (ed.), *Towards Self-Managing Schools*. London: Cassell, 1995.

WILLIAM J. CASILE *is director of the Leadership Institute and associate professor in the School of Education of Duquesne University. He is one of two principal investigators of the ASSET Teacher Enhancement Project in Pittsburgh, Pennsylvania.*

REENY D. DAVISON *is the executive director of ASSET Inc. and the other principal investigator of the ASSET Teacher Enhancement Project in Pittsburgh, Pennsylvania.*

Through the apparently intractable contemporary issues in Catholic schools in the United Kingdom, the author raises salient questions requiring consideration by leaders in all schools.

4

The ambiguity of moral leadership in Catholic schools

James Arthur

MUCH OF THE RECENT literature in educational administration has focused on understanding the human complexity of school leaders, particularly the moral nature of their role. There has also been a discernible movement away from the overtly rationalist approach, which often conceived leaders as essentially target setters and compilers of development plans (Day, 1995).

The increased use of religious metaphors for schools and educational leadership—terms such as *servant* and *shepherd*—reflects this growing concern with moral and ethical issues. A number of writers increasingly address the ideas of "moral commitment" in leadership and the promotion of visions and values that are shared and bind staff together with a collective understanding of purpose (Senge, 1990). Sergiovanni (1992) argues that leadership is an expression of an inner moral commitment to values and beliefs of such substance that it is these that lead, not the individual leaders themselves. He concludes that it is "the practice of fellowship [that] provides the basis of leadership." Starratt (1991) describes what an "ethical school" would look

NEW DIRECTIONS FOR SCHOOL LEADERSHIP, NO. 9, FALL 1998 © JOSSEY-BASS PUBLISHERS

like, while Greenfield (Greenfield and Ribbins, 1993, p. 225) believes that "schools are moral orders dedicated to a broad and significant set of values." These authors speak of leadership as visions that are created, communicated, and maintained by headteachers (principals) as part of the daily life of the school.

Hodgkinson (1991) views the headteacher as a philosopher as much as a person of action, taking actions that are above expediency and pragmatics. Significantly, he titled his book *Educational Leadership: The Moral Act*. Duignan and Bhindi (1997a, 1997b) consider the notion that "authentic leaders are spiritual leaders" and discuss the challenge this has for conventional leadership paradigms. All these authors claim that the moral and spiritual dimensions of leadership and the central place of the school community have been neglected in leadership studies. For them, values, morals, and ethics are at the center of leadership. They do not mean by this a religious understanding of moral and spiritual leadership, even though they employ religious language.

In contrast, one would assume that for a Catholic school the values underpinning its leadership would indeed largely be derived from religious belief. The Catholic "vision" or "mission" for education is of commitment to ethical absolutes that derive their authenticity from the moral nature of God and the church. Catholic headteachers therefore need to take seriously the substance of this religious view. An interesting development in leadership studies is that a number of the positions being advocated are strongly echoed in the Catholic view. Cahill (1994) found a high level of congruence between the thinking of authors cited earlier and Catholic educational ideals. In particular she surveyed the leadership writings of Greenfield (Greenfield and Ribbins, 1993) in relation to the education documents of the Second Vatican Council and found numerous points of connection.

Ethical ambiguities in leadership

Research by Byrk, Lee, and Holland (1993) in the United States concluded that there is a kind of leadership informed by "an inspirational ideology" that makes Catholic schools qualitatively different from other types of school. The emphasis here is on the spiritual and moral dimensions of leadership, for the Catholic conception of education is primarily religious. Byrk, Lee, and Holland also assert that it is the underlying values of the Catholic school that are shared by its members that provide the "animating force for the entire enterprise." Grace's (1996) research among Catholic headteachers in England found that they endorsed this view. His findings raised a number of key questions, not least of which being What direction do Gospel values give to the purpose and leadership within Catholic schools? Does it involve a form of biblically based leadership? There appears to be much confusion over exactly which Gospel values are adopted and promoted in Catholic schools—there is no universal consensus and Vatican II and its subsequent reports did not use the term. Grace also notes that "Post Vatican II Catholicism has resulted in greater realisation of ambiguity and paradox in moral codes. Leadership in Catholic schools is a continuing struggle with these ambiguities." Certainly, secular determinants of attitudes, beliefs, and values are commonplace in Catholic schools, which has led to a sense of ambiguity regarding the very identity of the church.

This secularization process sits uneasily alongside a leadership role that is intimately bound up with the development of a set of church values and beliefs. It poses a huge challenge for the headteacher's leadership, particularly when the very intelligibility of the church's teachings are often questioned by staff and pupils alike. As in most state schools, one cannot assume a consensus on values in and between Catholic schools. This leaves the headteacher and teachers to decide what values each should adopt, communicate, and promote.

"Dualism" in leadership

In England and Wales, recent evidence from the Office For Standards in Education (OFSTED) illustrates that Catholic schools are more likely to be rated highly by school inspectors—especially in their academic outcomes. This implies that they are effective schools with strong leadership. But what is the nature of this leadership and does it help us understand what kind of leadership is called for in Catholic schools? Despite their acknowledged secular success there are a number of factors that can be deduced about contemporary Catholic schools that may be pushing the leadership style found in them toward a "dualistic model" of Catholic leadership (Arthur, 1995a).

The dualistic model separates the role of the leader, both conceptually and practically, into two elements. First, the normal leadership and administrative functions common to all headteachers apply. Second, the additional religious and moral responsibilities and duties specific to headteachers of church schools come into play. For many headteachers the religious leadership role is perceived simply as a set of additional responsibilities. In the dualistic model there is no concerted attempt to integrate the moral and spiritual dimensions with general management policies adopted in the school. Before exploring the moral and spiritual dimensions of the Catholic headteacher's leadership role, it is important to review some major problems facing the recruitment of headteachers to Catholic schools in England.

Problematic trends in England and Wales

The number of applications for headteacher posts in Catholic schools is in a decline. Research by Howson (1989; 1996–1997) indicates that this is also the case for deputy headteachers (assistant principals). Some schools have so few applicants that they are unable to compile a short list of candidates to interview for appointment. Repeat advertisements for headteacher posts in Catholic schools are more than double the national rate and in secondary (high) schools they are more than three times this rate. The standard rate for readvertisement in 1996–97 was 14 percent for all state schools, but in Catholic secondary schools it was 48 percent. In Catholic primary (elementary) schools it was 24 percent.

Coupled with these figures is a continuing decline in the number of newly qualified Catholic teachers employed in Catholic schools. Catholic Colleges of Higher Education no longer accept that their central aim is the supply of Catholic teachers for Catholic schools and therefore the majority of teachers employed in Catholic secondary schools are trained outside the Catholic sector of teacher training. The number of Catholic teachers on the staff of Catholic schools is also in decline. The percentage of Catholic teachers working in Catholic secondary schools is now under 55 percent. This statistic alone has resulted in greater emphasis being placed on the quality of the leadership role in Catholic schools, on the mistaken basis that a strong Catholic ethos is created by the quality of the leadership. While the Catholic Church recognizes that there is a growing crisis, it has to date been unable to respond effectively.

Positional leaders: Appointment and role

In Catholic schools, headteachers are widely acknowledged to be crucial in defining the nature and quality of the religious life. Consequently, there is a growing emphasis by governors and diocesan officials on defining the religious and moral leadership qualities of Catholic headteachers. That they are expected to promote the religious identity and life of the school is illustrated by a memorandum approved by the Westminster Council for Diocesan Affairs in 1989 titled *Description and Responsibilities of Headteachers of a Catholic School*. Three principal responsibilities are detailed:

- First, potential headteachers need to understand the nature and purpose of Catholic education.
- Second, they must establish and sustain the Catholic identity of the school and safeguard the church's teaching on a day-to-day basis.
- Third, they must be leaders of a Catholic faith community comprising teachers and pupils.

This is a definition of community interpreted not as a sociological term but primarily as a theological concept and the only conditions for establishing such a faith community are achieved within a shared perspective of meaning. This represents a considerable challenge to headteachers of Catholic schools, who are charged with the responsibility of helping prepare pupils for adult membership of the church in conjunction with the wider Catholic community.

The appointment of headteachers is the responsibility of the governors in Catholic schools in England, and the Trust Deed for each school will usually make it clear that a Catholic must be appointed. The governors invariably consult with officials from the diocesan education commission who represent the interests of the trustees and are almost always present at the interviewing of candidates for appointment. There are also growing numbers of cases of dismissal, suspension, and governor difficulties over the appointment and retention of Catholic headteachers. Many of these have reached the national press or the courts in one form or another. Catholic headteachers certainly face a range of ethical and moral dilemmas. It is not surprising that research among headteachers conducted by Grace (1995) concluded, "Many of the dilemmas that the headteachers faced arose from a disjunction between official moral teaching and the mores of contemporary society."

Surprisingly, the majority of appointed headteachers of Catholic schools in England have never undertaken a systematic course in Catholic pastoral theology, philosophy, or psychology in preparation for their school leadership roles. It may sound astonishing, but very few such courses for Catholic teachers exist. As a result, teachers' knowledge of church documents and church teaching on education and social matters is uneven and diverse, often depending on personal interest. Nevertheless, they are employed to be leaders of the Catholic community in church schools. What governors may forget is that the institutional value system within Catholic schools can be a powerful influence on new headteachers and that a Catholic ethos will influence the kind of leadership that the headteacher offers. If there is a close symbiotic relationship, then a headteacher will find it easier to bond together with the staff in a common cause.

Vision becomes a reality through shared values, and if a headteacher is to lead effectively then the values of the school community must be congruent with those of the leader. This cause-and-effect relationship between followers and leaders has serious implications for Catholic schools. There needs to be a critical mass of Catholic believers who seek to motivate the rest of the school community and assist the headteacher in shaping the values of the school. Byrk, Lee, and Holland (1993) insist that leaders must be committed to and compatible with the "communal aims" of the school community. The appointment of new Catholic teachers is, therefore, just as important as the selection of a headteacher as a new school leader. Research in the United States by Diamond (1997) supports this view, since he found that the Catholic leader's self-efficacy depends on a high percentage of Catholic staff. Homogeneity among staff (faculty) over religious views was essential for the headteacher's leadership. However, there are a number of vital issues surrounding the ability and willingness of leaders in Catholic schools to promote particular Catholic values.

Leadership:
Ethical issues

The overwhelming majority of headteachers are believing and practicing Catholics, but many find difficulty with, or even may not accept, some of the authentic moral teachings of the church. They share with the wider Catholic community some degree of uncertainty about Catholic teaching on a whole range of issues: divorce, remarriage, sexuality, relationships outside marriage, and pregnancy outside marriage, to name some of the most obvious. While they accept that schools are moral agencies, they may find it difficult to perceive themselves as moral agents, which increases the ambiguity in their leadership role. Some Catholic headteachers also adopt a leadership style no different from their secular counterparts and display little in the way of Catholic distinctiveness in their leadership of the school's curriculum, finance, resources, or staff. This has led Brennan (1987) to suggest that there are only ordinary *schools* with Catholic headteachers. He asserts: "Unless the school, therefore, can come forward with a reasoned philosophy, distinctive and Gospel-based, which answers the demand that 'the essential work of the Catholic school is to translate effectively the truths of the religious lesson into the religious and academic, social and administrative structure of the school,' then we must stop claiming that we have Catholic schools with Catholic headteachers." The recent introduction and current development of the National Professional Qualification for Headteachers (NPQH) and the provision of training for serving headteachers offers Catholic authorities an unprecedented opportunity to address some of these important issues.

The development of a Catholic NPQH

Set within the education context of England and Wales, the national Teacher Training Agency has accredited regional providers of headteacher courses that will be assessed against national standards it has issued for headship of schools. Specific Catholic NPQH courses are being established that attempt to reflect the moral and spiritual concerns the church has about educational leadership in its schools since there are no requirements in the standards that are unique to Catholic school leaders. Nevertheless, the new national qualification for the preparation of aspiring headteachers can be tailored to meet Catholic needs if it is extended beyond the existing technical and administrative content. To provide indicators of outcomes that might be expected from a Catholic program in preparation for headship of Catholic schools the following list, although not intended to be exhaustive, provides a flavor of what these distinctive Catholic moral and spiritual values would look like:

Headteachers who are committed, believing, and practicing
    Catholics who pray in faith and are loyal to the church, accepting

its authentic teaching, and who can lead the school community
in prayer

Headteachers who insist on the central place of religion in the life of
the school community and ensure the priority of religious education on the timetable, school worship, and priestly chaplaincy

Headteachers who establish a school community where the process
of faith and moral development are integrated and where
Catholic social principles are embedded in the curriculum and
the life of the school

Headteachers who can articulate the Catholic educational vision of
the school and confidently expound a philosophy of Catholic
education and who can inspire in the school community a vision
of what it can become

Headteachers who see all things in the light of faith and place Christ
at the center of education and who can set the school tone
accordingly—and in particular, who are sensitive to the demands
of justice, love, and charity

It could be argued that every staff member in a school should
be expected to acquire and promote these values, not simply the
headteacher. This would sit well with Sergiovanni's description of
leadership. Preparation programs for leadership need therefore to
help shape not only the thoughts of Catholic teachers but also
their perceptions, beliefs, assumptions, emotions, and commit-
ments. It is a kind of seminary formulation that will demand more
than a secular standards course that has simply been adapted to
accommodate some Catholic concerns. Bradley's (1996) organizational structure of "shepherd leadership" provides an interesting
description of what a Christian school would look like. She lists
seven characteristics:

- A strong unity of purpose around a central vision
- A commitment to individual growth in the context of commu-
  nity
- A sense of belonging
- A recognition of functions differentiated according to abilities

- A view of appointed status as irrelevant
- A sense of shared responsibility
- A sense of interdependence among members

A Catholic school model

In this model the whole school community becomes one dynamic unit, interrelated, interconnected, and interdependent. This view of leadership is more organic than organizational. Leaders are essentially the servants of the needs of people in the faith-community and of the moral idea that binds them together. Sergiovanni (1992) believes that leaders, meaning all teachers, go beyond the call of duty because they have such high levels of commitment that the work itself is satisfying and self-actualizing.

In this model of Catholic schooling, practicing Catholic teachers who share the values of the school community are given priority in staff appointments. As Grace (1996) observes, this spiritual dimension of their leadership manifests itself in the language used by leaders in Catholic schools to describe their work. The religious ethos of the school is central to the Catholic school and a school with a strong ethos will be led by those who enunciate a moral character ideal, who respect the dignity of each person and have a commitment to caring and promoting social ethics. The role of governors and diocesan officials is to appoint leaders who have the capacity to motivate others to become committed to this shared vision and its goals. Essentially, governors need to appoint headteachers who can bridge the gap between a rich rhetoric and reality.

Contemporary issues

The problem is that aspiring headteachers in England and Wales may see many of these Catholic values as separate from their ordinary school leadership role, thus establishing a dual function approach to Catholic school leadership. Many of these values are already established in Catholic headteacher competency programs of preparation in the United States (Buetow, 1988). In a detailed evaluation of specific Catholic competencies in the United States, Parkes (1997) found that participants believed that the competencies in "faith development" were most important, while least important was "institutional management."

By contrast, the dual function approach to leadership in Catholic schools in England and Wales has facilitated the easy entry of the language of the quasi-markets that have been imposed on schools. The church describes the school as a faith community, but today many believe it to be little more than a business enterprise. In recent years, the education system appears to view knowledge as a commodity to be bought and sold—as opposed to knowledge viewed as service, not to be acquired for power or wealth. Knowledge seen as property to be selected and promoted according to its exchange value in the market is gaining an ascendancy while knowledge used as a means of self-fulfillment in order to develop cultural and social responsibility appears to be in decline.

Increasingly, headteachers are praised for their entrepreneurial skills in hiring out school property or managing schools as businesses, while less attention is focused on headteachers as leaders of educational communities. Students are viewed as units of resource or clients or customers rather than as unique individuals endowed with reason and conscience. Schools are also encouraged to view other schools as competitors or even as opponents. Schools are not encouraged to emphasize collectivity, collegiality, cooperation, and sharing. Education is also being steadily privatized—"voluntary" contributions extracted from parents effectively blur what the state should provide—which undermines education as a basic human right provided with guaranteed freedom of access. Catholic schools and Catholic headteachers have not been immune from these developments—indeed, some have eagerly engaged with them. Perhaps it would be prudent for everyone to reflect on Hodgkinson's injunction (1991) that "leaders must be guided by more than pragmatism, philistinism, and careerism."

The main policies of the existing education system in England and Wales appear to be geared explicitly to a utilitarian approach designed principally for future employment opportunities. Promoting religious and educational values, and not those of the market, should be the clear responsibility of the Catholic school and that of all other schools in England and Wales. The headteacher and staff should not simply be understood as professionals whose contribution is limited to the transmission of knowledge. Emphatically, they are also educators who help in the development and shaping of the human person. If Catholic religious principles had been integrated with the academic, administrative, and social aspects of schooling to form strong underlying fundamental values, they would have represented a major challenge to market forces. In the event, no such challenge has been made—beyond a rhetoric disconnected from the reality of Catholic schools.

Conclusion

The moral and spiritual leadership of followers as well as leaders is essential for the development of a Catholic school ethos. It is an "inspirational ideology" that can only succeed if there are enough committed Catholic teachers and pupils in Catholic schools who freely share Catholic moral and spiritual principles and values. Leadership is important, but it requires a critical mass of believing teachers who are themselves coleaders of school communities. The demands of Catholic headteacher preparation programs will obviously attract religiously committed teachers and will almost certainly deter other candidates with more secular leadership tendencies.

If the reported decline in applicants for school leadership appointments continues, the Catholic Church in England and Wales can therefore expect further decline in the number of teachers who are able to offer themselves for such preparation. The moral and spiritual requirements for aspiring headteachers are certainly major reasons for the decline in applications for Catholic headships. If sensitively handled, the NPQH could provide one means by which more aspiring headteachers will be available for governors to choose. However, the future of Catholic schools requires that an alternative and specifically Catholic approach to leadership courses be adopted that are open to all staff in Catholic schools and that emphasize values formation in residential diocesan centers. These programs may be seen as a prerequisite for admission to an NPQH course. They would include a systematic course in pastoral theology and would provide a church context for the often vague references to "Gospel values" in school. The courses would also be open and suitable for school governors who share the leadership role with all the teachers in a Catholic school.

Continued church support for more than 2,000 Catholic schools in England and Wales is dependent on the nurturing of Catholic educational leaders who are able to cope with the increasing ambiguity of their moral leadership. The church needs to find, enlist, train, and support teachers who share its value system and who are prepared to play their part in the leadership of the Catholic faith community. Failure in this critically important area may result in highly praised schools, but schools that lack the dimension of faith that makes them distinctive communities with an "inspirational ideology." As Grace (1996) believes: "Religious-educational cultures of many traditions carry messages about leadership that stand in a critical relation to those currently dominant or rising to dominance in secular culture. These traditions give pre-eminence to the spiritual and moral responsibilities of leadership, to notions of vocation in education and ideas of commitment relatively independent of reward or status. The extent to which these ideas are realised in practice by the leaders of religious schools is an empirical question of great interest and relevance for the various faith communities and others."

References

Arthur, J. *The Ebbing Tide: Policy and Principles of Catholic Education.* Leominster, England: Gracewing, 1995a.

Bradley, Y. "Old Wine, New Wineskins: Reflections on Metaphors for Christian Organisation." *Journal of Christian Education*, 1996, *39* (2).

Brennan, J. A. "The Catholic Headteacher and the Local Community." *The Month*, 1987, May.

Buetow, H. A. *The Catholic School: Its Roots, Identity, and Future.* New York: Crossroad, 1988.

Byrk, A., Lee, V., and Holland, P. *Catholic Schools and the Common Good.* Cambridge, Mass.: Harvard University Press, 1993.

Cahill, W. P. "Why Greenfield? The Relevance of T. B. Greenfield's Theories to Catholic Education." *Educational Management and Administration,* 1994, *22* (4).

Day, C. "Leadership and Professional Development: Developing Reflective Practice." In H. Busher and R. Saran (eds.), *Managing Teachers as Professionals in Schools.* London: Kogan Page, 1995.

Diamond, D. E. "An Analysis of Leadership Behavior and Self-Efficacy of Principals of Catholic Secondary Schools." Unpublished Ph.D. dissertation, Catholic University of America, 1997.

Duignan, P., and Bhindi, N. "Authenticity in Leadership: An Emerging Perspective." *Journal of Educational Administration,* 1997a, *35* (3).

Duignan, P., and Bhindi, N. "Leadership for a New Century." *Educational Management and Administration,* 1997b, *25* (2).

Grace, G. *School Leadership: Beyond Educational Management.* London: Falmer Press, 1995.

Grace, G. "Leadership in Catholic Schools." In T. McLaughlin, J. O'Keefe, and B. O'Keefe (eds.), *The Contemporary Catholic School: Context, Identity and Diversity.* London: Falmer Press, 1996.

Greenfield, T. B., and Ribbins, P. *Greenfield and Educational Administration: Towards a Humane Science.* London: Routledge, 1993.

Hodgkinson, C. *Educational Leadership: The Moral Act.* Albany: State University of New York, 1991.

Howson, J. "Report on Headteacher Turnover in Roman Catholic Schools in England and Wales." Unpublished paper, Oxford, Oxford Brookes University, 1989. Additional reports for 1996–97 have been used from the same source.

Parkes, J. D. "Perceptions of the Importance and Value of Catholic School Leadership Competencies." Unpublished Ph.D. dissertation, Boston College, 1997.

Senge, P. *The Fifth Discipline.* New York: Doubleday, 1990.

Sergiovanni, T. J. *Moral Leadership: Getting to the Heart of School Improvement.* San Francisco: Jossey-Bass, 1992.

Starratt, R. J. "Building an Ethical School: A Theory for Practice in Educational Leadership." *Educational Administration Quarterly,* 1991, *27* (2).

JAMES ARTHUR *is professor of education at Canterbury Christ Church College, Canterbury, United Kingdom.*

Broad-based public concern over the decline of values and character in society provides both challenges and opportunities for the leadership of schools and staff in their roles of teaching character education.

5

Leadership beyond the curriculum: The role of the school community in character education

James E. Antis

NEAR THE END of the nineteenth century, America was growing with rapid industrialization and urbanization. This growth was linked to a breakdown of influence by the church and family as sanctioning institutions of morality (Yulish, 1980). The trend continued throughout the first three decades of the twentieth century, when character education began to capture the attention of American educators. Along with the escalation of industrialization and urbanization, other factors such as an upsurge in immigration, World War I, and the spirit of the Roaring Twenties heightened the perception among the general population, and educators in particular, that social stability was being threatened and there was a growing need to reestablish moral standards.

Schools made attempts to integrate codes of conduct stressing right living, self-control, good health, kindness, sportsmanship, self-reliance, duty, reliability, truth, good workmanship, and teamwork into all

NEW DIRECTIONS FOR SCHOOL LEADERSHIP, NO. 9, FALL 1998 © JOSSEY-BASS PUBLISHERS

aspects of school life. These dates correspond to a trend identified by Leming (1993) and McClellan (1992), which indicated that during the 1920s and 1930s, schools were focusing on character development as an educational goal. More recently, the 1980s and early 1990s have witnessed a revival of the character education initiative.

Recent developments

A revival of interest in character education is currently taking place in our country. Cohen (1995) stated that character educators today are responding to the public's perception of a moral decline of America's social and cultural life. Tom Likona (1991), a noted author and authority on moral education, agrees that we are seeing the beginnings of a new character education movement that will restore good character to its historical place as a desirable outcome of schooling. Likona contends that schools cannot be ethical bystanders as our society struggles. Greenhalgh (1990) implored the cooperative efforts of scholars, practitioners, government, and the church to seek solutions to these difficult questions, as they become more and more evident in our pluralistic society.

This writer believes that it is equally as important to enhance the goodness of children as it is to enhance their "smartness." Although related, these are two different aspects in child development and we need to approach both in a purposeful way. As educators, we need to be concerned about the whole child. Moral development is a critical aspect of human growth. Educators need to respond and assume the dual responsibility of working with children to develop character as well as intellect. This purposeful approach to teaching virtue needs to become part of every school's mission. Our schools labor courageously to provide a high-quality education for today's youth amid the influence of growing societal ills.

The teaching of character should be an integral component embracing every aspect of the school community. As school administrators and teachers, it is our role to assume leadership in these areas. Akin, Dunne, Palomares, and Schilling (1995), in answering the question of why there is a need to educate for character, stated that children are growing up without a moral compass. Early and Gibbs (1993) referred to the past when it could be assumed that the home, church, synagogue, or community at large would instill traditional moral values in children. This can no longer be assumed today. Schools have therefore been placed in a position to have a tremendous influence on a child's moral development. Next to the home, schools have the best environment to teach the attributes of character that will keep children and the future of our society strong and stable. How then do we successfully accomplish the task?

School leadership

By the nature of our profession, educators have always had the opportunity, and most feel compelled, to share a sense of what is right and wrong with young people. Generally, the public believes it appropriate for educators to teach ethical behavior as long as the values taught are universally accepted and not indoctrinated (Goode, 1989). Johnson and Immerwahr (1994), in a report based on an in-depth public opinion study, discovered that overwhelming majorities of Americans across the nation believe that it is highly appropriate for public schools to teach universal values. It was also found important to do so in a manner that not only instills the knowledge but also produces behavior in children that demonstrates this knowledge in action. The goal then is for educators to disseminate moral knowledge in a universally acceptable way without offending the primacy of parents in their sense of responsibility in these matters.

Character education programs are becoming more and more prevalent in our schools in an attempt to turn the tide of societal decay. A number of these ethics education programs have emerged in an attempt to instill moral knowledge and enable students to translate this knowledge into moral action. These programs, often through use of quality literature, incentive programs, and other related activities, help children understand values such as respect, responsibility, honesty, justice, courage, loyalty, and other character-related concepts. These programs are designed to foster moral literacy and ethical judgment by teaching children to understand these concepts. Children are encouraged to learn about these concepts and then apply the learned concepts in their daily lives.

Leadership in the school

As educational leaders, it is our responsibility to be attuned to the moral atmosphere in our schools and to set a tone that positively motivates the entire school community. If we don't care as school leaders, why should anyone else? School culture regarding character development can be influenced by setting clear behavioral expectations.

Traditionally, the primary objective of our schools is to educate children in the academic content areas. Returning to the premise that it is equally important to enhance the goodness in children as it is to enhance their smartness, common sense tells us that we cannot succeed in our academic instructional goals and responsibilities without first establishing a moral climate in the school and classroom. The heart of any school is the classroom. The teacher, as classroom leader, is the key ingredient in establishing classroom moral atmosphere.

Greenhalgh (1990), investigating the moral atmosphere of schools, sought to identify aspects of school life that contributed to the moral climate. These aspects centered on the teaching and modeling of respect, the importance of leadership, teacher commitment, and the creation of a moral community in the classroom and in the school. He concluded that there were definite variables that had an effect on school atmosphere. Two of the most significant findings were the need for principals to recognize that their leadership of the school has a clear moral dimension, and the need for teachers to recognize that their commitment to positive moral development of their students was also significant in this regard.

A study by this writer, evaluating the impact of a character education program on ethical understanding, ethical sensibility, and ethical behavior of elementary children (Antis, 1997), confirmed the variables identified by Greenhalgh. In this study, *ethical understanding* referred to the ability of children to understand character-related concepts, *ethical sensibility* to the child's sense of doing the right thing when confronted with a moral decision, and *ethical behavior* to the application or actual physical response to a situation requiring moral action. Modeling character-related concepts by adults was part of the integration process and a factor in determining the effect of the program on the school community. The principal assumed responsibility and primary leadership for the character initiative and provided support for the faculty in their implementation efforts. The principal's commitment to leadership of the initiative involved planning activities, communicating to parent and community groups, providing staff development, and ensuring follow-up support and accountability through supervision. The use of character-related vocabulary permeated communication between adults and children. There was a commitment to all aspects of the school program.

The results of the study clearly indicated that the character education program had a positive impact on children for the variables indicated. Both qualitative and quantitative results reinforced and confirmed the positive impact of the school's leadership in the wealth of evidence found in comments and observations of parents, teachers, principals, and students from the experimental school participating in the study.

Leadership in the community

School leadership also has a role in the community at large in justifying the importance of implementing character education programs in the schools. The introduction of ethics education programs has at times met with strong opposition from community sources due to the concern that schools were infringing on the responsibilities of parents in values education. The school leader must provide a methodical and well-planned introduction and implementation process and communicate this message to the community.

A key factor to the success of a character education initiative is to provide an "up front" approach, emphasizing the teaching of universal values that are not in conflict with religious or other personal values typically taught in the home. Parents, school district administration, and the governing board must continually be informed of program content, goals, and methods of implementation. In his handbook on the development of a character education program, Huffman (1994) emphasized the importance of the school leader, or "executive champion," in creating an atmosphere of openness and trust within the community. He stressed the need to have an action plan to communicate with critical audiences and discussed the importance of modeling the core values of the program.

Teachers often grow wary when character education becomes a purposeful part of the school's mission. They become fearful, in a sense, of how parents might react to their efforts to instill values in their children. Actually, there is nothing teachers and administrators do in school that is values-neutral (Akin, Dunne, Palomares, and Schilling, 1995). Choice of words, tone of voice, actions, behaviors, and treatment of others all send messages to children about how a person ought to think and behave. Open communication with parents and the community will build a sense of trust in the teacher's efforts to implement the program.

Owens (1992), in a study of teacher perspectives on teaching values, concluded that teachers in general believe that teaching values is an integral part of their responsibility as educators, and that it is important for school administrators to take the lead in relieving teachers of possible confrontation from members of the public. It is critical that school leaders reassure teachers that they have administrative support and the community that the school's intentions are honorable. The school leadership must assure the staff that they will not be alone if a problem develops. If teachers sense that they will not have the support of administration, they will not pursue character education in a purposeful manner. My own study (Antis, 1997) also confirmed these findings. School leadership strategies are critical in setting the stage for success of any program.

Conclusion

School leaders have been placed in a position to have tremendous influence on a child's moral growth. The current resurgence of teaching for character has become a noteworthy crusade in our schools. It is important that, as educational leaders and responsible members of society, we are not discouraged by what seems to be an overwhelming task of instilling traditional values in our youth. The underlying issue is the need for responsible parenting and the setting of priorities by those who are in a position to influence decision making in areas that can produce societal change. As educational leaders in the twenty-first century, each of us has a sphere of influence that can make this change in the life of a child or in the making of a positive difference in some way in our own community.

Along with efforts from home to develop a child's knowledge and ability to tell right from wrong, the school provides an ideal environment and opportunity to teach the attributes of character to children that will restore a strong and stable direction for the future of our society.

References

Akin, T., Dunne, G., Palomares, S., and Schilling, D. *Character Education in America's Schools*. Spring Valley, CA: Innerchoice, 1995.

Antis, J. F. "An Evaluation of the Effect of a Character Education Program on the Ethical Understanding, Ethical Sensibility, and Ethical Behavior of Elementary Children." Unpublished doctoral dissertation, Duquesne University, Pittsburgh, Pa., 1997.

Cohen, P. "The Content of Their Character." *Association for Supervision and Curriculum Development Curriculum Update*, Spring 1995, pp. 1–8.

Early, E. J., and Gibbs, L. J. "Character Education: A Noble Cause in Search of a Noble Audience." *Journal of the Pennsylvania School Boards Association*, 1993, *59* (1), 12–17.

Goode, S. "A Growing Call for Teaching Values." *Insight*, 1989, pp. 56–59.

Greenhalgh, D. C. "Investigating the Moral Atmosphere of Schools." Unpublished doctoral dissertation, Boston University, Boston, Mass., 1990.

Huffman, H. A. *Developing a Character Education Program: One School District's Experience*. Alexandria, Va.: Association for Supervision and Curriculum Development, The Character Education Partnership, 1994.

Johnson, J., and Immerwahr, J. *First Things First: What Americans Expect from the Public Schools*. New York: Public Agenda, 1994.

Leming, J. S. "In Search of Effective Character Education." *Educational Leadership*, 1993, *51*, 63–71.

Likona, T. *Educating for Character: How Our Schools Can Teach Respect and Responsibility*. New York: Bantam, 1991.

McClellan, B. E. "Schools and the Shaping of Character: Moral Education in America, 1607–Present." ERIC Clearinghouse for Social Studies/Social

Science Education and the Social Studies Development Center, Indiana University, 1992.

Owens, R. C., Jr. "Teacher Perceptions Concerning Their Role and The Efficacy of Moral Education in Public Elementary Schools." Unpublished doctoral dissertation, Iowa State University, 1992.

Yulish, S. M. *The Reach for a Civic Religion: A History of the Character Education Movement in America, 1890–1935.* Washington, D.C.: University Press of America, 1980.

JAMES E. ANTIS *is assistant superintendent of schools in the Indiana Area School District, Indiana, Pennsylvania, and former principal of an elementary school in Indiana, Pennsylvania.*

Drawing on research data from a group of schools in England and Wales, the author emphasizes the necessity for school leaders to show clear educational purpose, conceptual responsiveness to mandated innovation, and acceptance of the need to modify organizational structures to develop collaborative partnerships in schools and communities they serve.

6

School leadership in a reformed educational environment

Graham Deeks

The 1988 Education Reform Act (ERA) was a systemic watershed in the development of the education system in England and Wales in an amalgam of many complex and often controversial elements. For many educators, the Act reflected a series of paradoxes exposing extreme positions and provoking controversial debate.

Post-1988:
A decade of organizational and cultural change

Inexorably, ERA was introduced as the means by which schools could be more efficiently controlled by central government through the application of market forces to the education system. It introduced the National Curriculum, which would be assessed and compared

NEW DIRECTIONS FOR SCHOOL LEADERSHIP, NO. 9, FALL 1998 © JOSSEY-BASS PUBLISHERS

nationally. A site-based management system known as Local Management of Schools (LMS) in England and Wales is an essential part of the plan, designed to give schools new individual authority within a centrally imposed policy of individual school accountability. This system is the means through which schools become self-managing with unprecedented degrees of autonomy, both in terms of budget and organization.

The mandated center-periphery management approach gave individual schools freedom in terms of self-determination, management, and ability to prioritize needs. On the other hand, the central role played by governing boards of schools was a major change in school governance in the 1980s and 1990s and schools were required to accept a prescribed curriculum, nationally designed and assessed. If schools were assessed as failing by centrally imposed benchmarks or prescribed performance indicators such as pupil attainment targets, training levels, or staff appraisal levels, they would be publicly censured, and, in extreme cases, possibly closed.

It was in this post-1988 climate that primary (elementary) schools had to address the central issue of how to best manage these mandated changes. Headteachers (principals), teachers, governors, and parents all had significant roles to play in the change process, not least because the creation of a consumer-oriented education system had ensured that market principles were now applicable to schools. School self-management had necessitated increased teacher and governor involvement and awareness of all new management responsibilities.

A major cultural upheaval required by the demands of LMS and a move away from hierarchical management principles to more collaborative styles was signaled by the legislation. The 1988 ERA presented schools with important choices as well as major problems. To cope adequately with all the mandated changes and flourish by adopting them, primary schools needed to recognize teaching staff as *the* major resource to be harnessed within the school. Individuals needed to be encouraged to participate, to increase their own knowledge and skill levels, and to receive in-service curriculum and management training. Ideally, they needed to be shown that they should collaborate in creating a new vision of the school through the transformation of its organizational structure and culture.

Implementation of mandated change

The ways in which schools and key positional leaders within them reacted and responded to the changes imposed by the Act were clearly critical to the achievement of the more effective education system it was intended to create. Reactions to the introduction of LMS provide useful examples. In England and Wales LMS has been mandated for all state-funded schools and is considerably more extensive and complex than site-based management policies and systems found elsewhere. Initial concern existed over both LMS and the simultaneously mandated National Curriculum, which might be accepted by schools either willingly and in a spirit of mutual hope and enthusiasm, or unwillingly through a sense of coercion based on mistrust and disapproval of governmental motives. If the sweeping and unprecedented changes were managed badly, then it seemed likely not only that there would be substandard school performance but also that staff attitudes and purposeful whole-school cultures would deteriorate.

A further practitioner concern existed over the nature and pace of systemic and cultural change in that it would be of particular significance for primary schools because for most children they provide the first experience of formal education in a structured environment. It was also reasonable to presume that early school experience for students would color their attitudes to later educational opportunities, thereby giving a special psychological dimension and sociological importance to primary education. The importance of this special dimension had always been recognized by most primary schools in England and Wales and was reflected in the main recommendations of the influential mid-1960s Plowden Report, which emphasized the centrality of a school culture for child-centered education.

During the decade following the 1988 Act a systemic revolution has been implemented. The introduction of LMS in the primary sector, with its prioritization of both financial and teaching effectiveness together with a new orientation to consumer marketing, required major changes in primary school management and organization. These major innovations also highlighted the need for a radical review of current practices and procedures in school management for the development of new strategies and *in situ* training for headteachers and others likely to be involved in responding to fundamental changes.

Prior to 1990, primary school achievements had not been subjected to rigorous and regular external appraisal or interschool comparisons. However, with the introduction of school self-governance, an inescapable drive toward competitive conditions and increased levels of accountability made it necessary for all schools to examine their organizational and management structures.

Three key variable factors have had considerable impact on management of change processes in school, whether organizational or cultural or both. The key variables are:

- Level and quality of staff involvement
- Individual attitudes and perceptions
- Management style

To examine the influence of these key variables during change processes, an action research study involving the selection of twenty primary schools in a southern England Local Education Authority (LEA—broadly equivalent to large school districts in the United States) became the focus of a three-year research study.

Management of organizational and cultural change in schools

Over a three-year period extending to the middle of the decade, and following the implementation of the 1988 Education Act, data from the research survey produced an inventory of similarities and consistencies in the sample of primary schools. For example, in schools where staff involvement and participation were encouraged in at least one of three key areas, the activities extended into other areas of change. In two schools where teaching staff and members of the governing boards were consistently and routinely encouraged to become involved in school management there was genuine enthusiasm and commitment to strive for even greater educational effectiveness.

Although final survey data indicated that only five schools out of the twenty in the study had made demonstrable progress in terms of authentic effectiveness in seeking to manage real cultural change, eleven other schools had also recognized that they needed positively to "manage" change or at least seriously attempt to do so. The remaining four schools continued to operate hierarchical management systems; retaining their positional status was seen as most important by the headteachers in these schools.

The survey findings identified two areas that could assist in the achievement of school improvement and greater effectiveness. The first element was in the preparation for change at school level. The data indicated that governors, headteachers, and staff in primary schools believed they had not received adequate, relevant support and training to enable them to cope with the regulatory requirements that mandated the implementation of imposed educational change. From the perspective of the schools, LEA training programs relating to LMS procedures were deficient both in content and focus of the training. Important areas were dealt with superficially and the didactic nature of training programs ensured that levels of individual participation were minimal. Only two schools had introduced structured and planned in-school training in relation to LMS. The other schools were generally content to rely on headteacher dissemination involving little personal involvement.

The overall perception of preparation for LMS and its relationship to management of change issues indicated that there was a lack of awareness of the crucial role of training in relation to the facilitation of successful cultural and philosophical management and organizational changes. LMS training appeared to operate in a rather isolated fashion with little or no consideration given to other key management of change issues such as:

- Relating organizational and developmental planning to the concepts of LMS
- Examining concepts of market forces and making attitudinal adjustments to meet new expectations in both internal and external environments
- Encouraging the changing of boundaries of power and control and, consequently, individual roles within primary schools
- Examining the notion of practitioner accountability and appraisal as it affected individuals and the whole school

In effect, schools believed that the integral unity of LMS as a conceptual framework was not addressed in the training and the fundamental underpinnings and philosophical basis of LMS appeared not to have been considered. The acceptance of "ownership" of this major educational innovation as such appeared to be at risk in an environment where technical operation and practical details were given priority over underlying rationale and philosophy.

In the final phase of the research survey, the implementation of LMS occurred and was being managed by the primary schools with varying degrees of success. The preparation and training for LMS had provided opportunities for schools to make significant progress toward achieving cultural change. However, the data revealed that the majority of schools in the survey had failed to seize opportunities for cultural change and autonomous development.

The second area of major concern to emerge from the research findings focused on monitoring and evaluation. In terms of school management, this concept was not one previously recognized as essential in the development of effective primary school management practices and procedures. Certainly, it received no particular emphasis in the preparation and training provided for the introduction of LMS. Most schools in the research study relied on three categories of traditionally valued methods for monitoring and evaluating school policies: informal communication networks, shared perceptions at staff (faculty) meetings, and the cultivation of a positive school ethos.

From survey data it was evident that three schools had developed clear policies and practice in each category. They had also introduced structured monitoring and evaluation mechanisms into their management activities. Consultation, participation, and sharing in all the main management processes were integral to their monitoring and evaluation procedures. Positive outcomes, evident in levels of participation, enthusiasm, and understanding achieved by practitioners in these three schools, illustrated the value and importance of planning and implementing a structured and participative school management monitoring and evaluation scheme.

Planning for educational progress

The absence of opportunities for planned and purposeful monitoring and evaluation by staff and governors in most of the schools in the research study ensured that the intellectual and experiential resources of existing faculty members within schools were underutilized. Cyclical monitoring and evaluation, feedback, change, and improvement processes were conspicuously absent in most of the twenty primary schools studied in the survey. The reliance on traditional informal, unstructured, and unplanned monitoring and evaluation procedures did not provide confidence that improved school effectiveness would be achieved.

Thus two key areas—preparation for change and monitoring and evaluation of the mandated expectations—had not received sufficient, if any, attention from either the LEA or individual headteachers. Even more important, these deficiencies were recognized by most practitioners in the twenty survey schools. However, four schools saw no necessity for any major change in school management or culture under LMS. The other sixteen primary schools acknowledged, with varying degrees of insight and candor, that lack of consideration and training in preparation would lead to less effective implementation in the schools than they desired. Similarly, the dearth of preparation and training in the monitoring and evaluation of mandated change in curricular and organizational frameworks was likely to lead to schools being less effective than required.

For example, under regulatory processes of reform a specific disciplined and structured approach was required in the preparation of a school development plan (SDP) via the formulation of a precise definition of aims and objectives. Every school was required to produce an SDP that contained specific and planned objectives. The research study revealed that production of SDPs was dependent on individual headteachers because of the center-periphery dissemination policy of the LEA. Despite the availability of excellent planning guidelines from the Government Department for Education and Employment (DFEE), many headteachers in the study had not produced authentic SDPs.

Following staff and governor consultation leading to the formal adoption of strategic SDPs, preparations to translate broad educational planning into operational processes for teachers and students provided a natural sequence. Similarly, budgetary and organizational procedures to enable schools to achieve their stated goals were also articulated. Again, the influence of headteachers was paramount. In some schools headteachers had decided that only limited consultation with the teaching staff and school governors should take place.

The final operational phase at school level was the implementation of the process and procedures for the monitoring and assessment of educational progress to provide feedback to participants and members of the school's governing board. From reflection and analysis of outcomes, appropriate adjustments could be made to keep the programmed educational activities on course to meet the declared objectives. Once again, headteacher influence was critical—and it was disappointing to find that in most of the schools surveyed planned monitoring and assessment processes were perfunctorily undertaken or nonexistent.

New directions for school improvement:
Training and development for all professional leaders

Broadly, of several major conclusions derived from the three-year research study, the following points appear to be particularly relevant to school leadership issues during processes of mandated change:

- Cuban's much-quoted comment (1988) about "the rocks of flawed implementation" is seen as highly appropriate in the survey, where a major finding was that the preparation stage for the introduction of LMS in primary schools was generally inadequate, making "flawed implementation" almost inevitable. It was also clear that the addition of information and management skills programs specifically geared to self-governance of schools should become a centrally important element in future training programs.
- Although of limited geographical range and quantitative dimensions, the research study produced findings that clearly indicated that professional development should not be left to subjective judgments by individual school leaders. Further, when severe budgetary constraints exist—as during the preimplementation phase of LMS in England and Wales—provision for hands-on preparatory training for mandated change should be funded from central sources either by the LEA or via earmarked government programs.
- It is essential that practitioners who aspire to be headteachers receive training in modern management techniques and that appropriate in-service development programs should be made available to existing positional leaders. Two years following completion of this research study considerable progress in provision of training programs has been made. The government's Teacher Training Agency (TTA) has recently launched the National Professional Qualification for Headteachers (NPQH) to provide opportunities for headteacher training at accredited regional

centers in England and Wales. The TTA will determine national standards and monitor provision of training programs for existing and aspiring headteachers.

- Unsurprisingly, the disparate leadership and management styles of headteachers were central to school cultures. The study confirmed the pivotal role of the headteacher in all major school functions. However, the research revealed that some important management of change principles had been jeopardized by poor leadership or dictatorial personal styles.

- Collaboration and individual involvement are two critically important principles in the management of successful change. This study showed yet again that both factors had important influences on individual and collective teacher attitudes, which in turn enhanced or undermined subsequent innovative activities in several schools in the study. Equally, it was disappointing to find that other significant concepts such as empowerment, stakeholding, and delegation received little consideration in several of the primary schools visited. It is essential that in-service programs specifically incorporating these strategies should be made widely available to serving headteachers.

- Inevitably, the personalities and associated behaviors of headteachers were crucially significant. Preexisting attitudes toward change and leadership flexibility are always influential in that more enlightened headteachers will be popular with their colleagues and students and therefore find it easier to promote widespread collaboration in the schools they lead. Nevertheless, all headteachers need to be aware that positive approaches to collegial collaboration and individual involvement are required if the management of change is to be successfully negotiated and achieved.

During the period following the 1988 Education Act and the concomitant introduction of sweeping changes under the mandated requirements inherent in the adoption of the National Curriculum and LMS, organizational culture and internal management processes in most schools surveyed reflected long-established traditional practices.

The organizational structures within several schools had been determined by headteachers with little or no consultation with or collaboration between other grades of staff and the governors. Appropriately in the new context of self-managing schools, Williams (1995) examines organizational change and refers to political and positional power in the control of people and resources. In this study, only three schools fully involved all appropriate individuals in the development of organizational and decisional structures. This lack of consultation was accepted agreeably by a few respondents who were indifferent to concepts of consultation, but it was resented and caused bitterness among others who considered that they should have been consulted but were ignored.

Beyond the three schools just mentioned, individuals within other schools did not believe they were regarded by their head-teachers as being significant contributors in influencing or deter-mining the organizational culture of the school. Many concepts considered essential in successful management of change by writ-ers as diverse as Holly and Southworth (1989), Nias (1989), Senge (1990), and Fullan (1991)—genuine staff participation, faculty own-ership of the changes, individuals being valued and empowered stakeholders, and a culture of collegiality—were conspicuously absent. In the majority of schools surveyed none of these concepts, nor those of teams operating with shared vision, agreed objectives, and preplanned methods by which to achieve change, were posi-tively demonstrated. Only six schools could be seen as operating or attempting to operate with these principles in mind. Disappoint-ingly, only one school could, in the application of models for suc-cessful organizational development and cultural change, be described as a genuinely collaborative school—a condition attrib-utable to its exceptionally high level of individual involvement and interstaff cooperation.

Invariably, managing successful change necessitates a structured and well-developed monitoring and appraisal system within all schools. The informal and unstructured methods extensively used in most of the twenty schools were inadequate. The low priority accorded by headteachers to the need to check and control various teaching and learning activities was the usual reason advanced by schools that had introduced no structured evaluation and monitoring processes since the introduction of LMS. In fourteen of the twenty schools only informal, unstructured, and therefore potentially inefficient and ineffective monitoring and assessment occurred. In practice, this meant that little if any real evaluation of internal management structures and learning processes had occurred and could be considered significant during the research study.

Achievement of cultural and organizational change

In relation to attitudes to progressive cultural and organizational change, the research data produced three groups of schools. Crucial to all groups were the varying perceptions of headteachers, whose personal preferences were instrumental in deciding collective attitudes within each school.

- The first group of schools did not really consider that cultural change was necessary. Headteachers of these schools defended their no-change policy by claiming that teachers were so preoccupied with the National Curriculum that they had to be protected from any involvement with LMS practice and procedures. Headteachers in this group who were in catchment areas where the schools were already oversubscribed also believed that demographic indications for future enrollments were very favorable. In addition, as the school performance achievements were already recognized as being good, these headteachers felt largely immune from competitive market forces. Thus for these reasons no cultural or organizational changes were considered necessary. It is emphasized that these were essentially headteacher perspectives and were not necessarily endorsed or accepted by teachers within, and governors of, the schools. In this group, headteacher perspectives reflected a general lack of consultation with, and involvement of, faculty and members of governing boards.

- Within the second group several individuals, headteachers, faculty, and members of governing boards had accepted the need for a degree of cultural change even though the schools appeared to be relatively immune from adverse market forces because they were in favorable supply-demand locations. These schools had introduced positive efforts for increased staff involvement in collaborative endeavors to achieve successful change.

• In the third group a clear majority of respondents (headteachers, faculty, and members of governing boards) had recognized the value of and need for cultural change. Initial innovative procedures, modified practice, and organizational change in schools had been largely achieved during the period of research. The relatively few schools within this group were characterized by high levels of individual involvement of staff as professional leaders through collaborative and empowering management organization sustained by progressive headteachers. High-quality interpersonal collegiality in these schools was conducive to positive staff attitudes and planned systems for the continuous monitoring and assessment of learning activities.

Conclusions

Some enlightening conclusions from this survey showed similarities with recent work by Hargreaves (1995). He argues that communicating with parents is an essential aspect of widening the approach to educational change. He claims there are four types of relationships between parents and schools, and clear connections between his four types and the situations found the twenty schools surveyed can be made:

• *Market-based relationships:* These view parents and pupils as clients and consumers, and tend to be contractual relationships favoring the already advantaged schools.

• *Managerial relationships:* These presume that schools are rational organizations within a decentralized system. In the establishment of parent-councils and the formulation of SDP, the managerial approach is better at creating committees than in building genuine working groups.

- *Personal relationships between teachers and parents:* These concentrate on the most important interests that parents have in the school—the achievements and well-being of their own children. Deeper parent-teacher relationships require that principles of openness, trust, risk taking, and collaboration are explicitly recognized and incorporated in policies to enhance parent-school contact.

- *Cultural relationships:* These relationships are founded on principles of openness and collaboration developed collectively with groups of parents and others in the community as a whole. Schools often decide on their professional response first, then take a managerial approach to informing their community. Yet when schools involve communities in a shared enterprise, public assistance, support, and understanding are much more likely to exist.

Using terms suggested by Hargreaves, five of the schools in the study appear to have many of the characteristics of both the "personal relationships" and "cultural relationships" types. The emphasis on developing and improving external relationships was based on aspects such as shared visions and goals, involvement of staff and positive delegation, the creation of a common culture and high expectations, monitoring and assessment to focus on how well the school achieves its goals, and concentration on fostering home-school links.

These schools acknowledged that the educational system was increasingly influenced by a market environment and as a consequence a clear need existed to focus positively on what the school aimed to become and how its ethos would develop. The creation of a public relations approach to marketing the school did not, however, result in the schools' engaging in consumer conflict with other local schools. Rather they were content to endeavor to maximize their individual educational effectiveness and ensure well-designed publicity. All these schools were actively engaged in collaboration with other local schools with which they worked in concert for the establishment of strategies aimed at highlighting the excellence of the service provided to the community by all schools.

Six other schools appeared to fall under the umbrella of Hargreaves's "market-based relationships," but with features of "personal relationships" also being evident. The emphasis on pupil achievement in affluent socioeconomic environments has ensured that these schools, despite their reluctance to embrace external change, have continued to thrive as organizations.

Several of the remaining nine schools exhibited clear characteristics of the "managerial relationships" type with some features of the "personal relationships" type. The cultural emphasis within these schools appeared to be on structure and shape, rather than flexibility and vision. All external relationships of the school were absorbed within a single committee or distributed among several others and became assimilated in other school organizational issues, thus relegating these important functions to subordinate positions.

On balance, the research study clearly indicated the importance of school leaders' actively engaging the experience, skills, and insights of all stakeholders in educational enterprises. From this study of recent and continuing systemic educational change in England and Wales, it is evident that every school should actively cultivate leaders at every level within and beyond its internal organization and neighborhood community to develop cultures of mutually collaborative endeavor and to celebrate collective achievement.

References

Cuban, L. *The Managerial Imperative and the Practice of Leadership in Schools.* Albany: State University of New York Press, 1988.

Fullan, M. G. *The New Meaning of Educational Change.* London: Cassell, 1991.

Hargreaves, A. "Back to the Joy of Teaching." *Tines Educational Supplement,* Oct. 6, 1995, p. 18.

Holly, P., and Southworth, G. *The Developing School.* London: Falmer Press, 1989.

Nias, J. *Primary Teachers Talking: A Study of Teaching as Work.* New York: Routledge, 1989.

Senge, P. *The Fifth Discipline.* New York: Doubleday, 1990.

Williams, V. "Towards 2000: Organization and Relationships." In V. Williams (ed.), *Towards Self-Managing Schools.* London: Cassell, 1995.

GRAHAM DEEKS *is an educational consultant following completion of his D. Phil. degree at the University of Oxford.*

Currently, the education system in Israel is going through major changes with implications for school leadership as well as for the way schools perceive and interact with their environment.

7

The emerging role of school leadership in Israel: From external to internal locus of control

Ami Volansky, Avi Habinski

THE STATE OF ISRAEL was established in 1948 when the Jewish population numbered some 600,000 residents. Within less than a decade, during a period of financial austerity, the country absorbed about 1.2 million immigrants including survivors of the European Holocaust and newcomers mainly from North African and Middle Eastern countries. The foundations of the Israeli education system were established during these years. Values were identified and key goals were promoted. The focus was on equality, improved school attendance, and the transfer of the national heritage to young citizens. It was felt that a centralized system would be the most appropriate for a rapid response to address the extensive educational needs of the young country. Priority needs included the construction of new schools, the training of teachers, the development of curricula, and the preparation of learning resources.

NEW DIRECTIONS FOR SCHOOL LEADERSHIP, NO. 9, FALL 1998 © JOSSEY-BASS PUBLISHERS

The Compulsory Education Law of 1949 established the requirement that every child age five through thirteen should participate in the education process. It also identified a role for local authorities (including cities, municipalities, and regional districts) in partnership for the provision of educational services for residents within their jurisdiction. In reality, *partnership* meant that the local authority was required to offer school facilities and provide administrative and support services such as maintenance and custodial and secretarial services. The Ministry of Education concentrated on the pedagogical component of the educational provision and employed professionally qualified staff in schools to provide compulsory educational services for students in grades 1 through 8 with extension into higher grades in later years.

Local authorities were given freedom to determine the level of support they wished to provide for education services. The flexibility offered to local authorities was the first step in the development of an educational system in which wide disparities existed between affluent and poor communities in the determination of funding made available for educational provision.

In the early 1950s the Israeli government decided to support the request of the teachers' professional association that qualified staff in schools providing mandated education services should be recognized as employed personnel within the public service sector. Following agreement, the government's central office established national regulations and became involved in operational decisions such as the appointment of teachers and principals, the transfer and termination of teacher appointments, the determination of the levels of salaries for teachers and principals, conditions of employment and service, and professional development and in-service education of teachers. These developmetns were significant in the growth of a system of financial and regulatory dependency of state schools on the Ministry of Education and led, inexorably, to a culture of central control through directives and rules that gained momentum and spread to other areas of the Ministry's activities.

Under the State Education Law of 1953, an inspectorate was established. The Regulation of State Education (Inspection

Orders), 1956, defined the roles and responsibilities of official appointments with responsibility for managing the education system. The omission of the school principal from the Regulations, which described the roles and responsibilities of individuals in leadership positions in the educational system, pointed to the perception of a centralized system in which a school principal was essentially an operations person who would obey, follow, and implement certain directives.

A review of the formal roles of the inspectorate indicated only limited confidence in the ability of school principals to undertake leadership roles in the educational system and to represent the interests of schools in interaction with their environment. The establishment of the inspector role was clearly an attempt to introduce an element of accountability and external management of schools.

In the 1994 annual report of the State Comptroller, the onerous responsibilities of the general inspector were acknowledged. The report concluded that because of their excessively burdensome roles inspectors were unable to discharge their duties satisfactorily or effectively. One conclusion of the report was that as each general inspector was responsible for an average of ten schools, it would be more effective to delegate a measure of authority to and increase the operational autonomy of schools.

In discussing the centralized system, it is essential to mention the central control of initiatives in schools. The direct allocation of resources by the Ministry of Education to schools was undertaken through the allocation of weekly teaching hours based on the number of students in a class, and through the direct funding of projects.

In 1972, the concern about the impact of sweeping external initiatives was raised by a committee established by the Minister of Education. The committee recommended the encouragement of teacher-led initiatives and identified existing professional apathy, weariness, and even bitterness among teachers. It suggested that in such a centralized educational regime even the most dedicated teachers could lose interest, suffer low morale, and avoid taking personal responsibility in schools.

However, during the mid-1970s, the number of projects steadily increased and reflected new concepts introduced by politicians, senior department officials, and other interest groups. A recent study undertaken by the Ministry's evaluation unit, *A Thousand Flowers Will Bloom* (1997), is an analysis of the effects of external projects in schools in a single city in Israel.

Frequently, schools are faced with a dilemma. Should a school accept additional projects that provide extra resources and sometimes prestige at the expense of focusing on goals it has identified for its students and community? In addition to providing extra resources, most projects come with requirements—for example, a commitment to follow certain prescribed processes or to have staff and principal participate in programs for extended professional development. On occasion, vaguely defined goals applicable to any project are proposed for individual schools.

Another implication of this "project approach" is that schools do not always know whether the resources they receive are equitable and adequate. Much concern has been expressed over the possibility that a centralized allocation of educational development resources has widened disparities between schools perceived to be successful and those regarded as underachieving.

Further, schools that are skilled in presenting their applications for special projects and associated additional resources are likely to secure additional funding, whereas schools without such expertise, reputation, or access to influential networks are unlikely to attract special projects and additional resource funding. Criticism of the centralized patronage system (which led to a dependency network mainly controlled by school inspectors) was recognized as having major disadvantageous social, financial, and educational implications.

The earlier culture characteristic of a bureaucratic, hierarchical approach may be illustrated in the form of an equilateral triangle balanced on one angle. The school was located at the lowest point, while the local authority and the ministry occupied the other two points. The school received directives, instructions, and resources from both upper points. This approach—illustrated on the left of Figure 7.1—reflects a typical bureaucratic culture, which assumes

Figure 7.1. From External to Internal Locus of Control

that superior concepts, knowledge, wisdom, information, and leadership are located at the most senior status levels. It is here that those holding positional status assume that they know best what is required at the local community level. For the Israeli education service this basic assumption proved to be both inaccurate and inadequate in terms of educational provision for student teaching and learning in schools. In recent years it has been widely recognized that outstanding human resources—minds, talents, and skills—exist at school and community levels, where people are aware of local needs and skilled in many of the ways in which those requirements should be addressed.

A major effort has been made to invert the triangle as illustrated on the right of Figure 7.1, placing the schools at the apex. Here they would function as semi-autonomous decision-making units, key centers for growth and improvement in education provision. Important elements in the repsonsibilities of the ministry and local authorities are the creation of optimal frameworks for the success of the schools, and the provision of support, so that they could achieve the goals they set for their students and communities. The following section summarizes current policies in action and evaluates progress to date.

Toward internal school management: The Israeli model of self-managing schools

The Israeli education system is one of the few continuing to preserve the historical inspection approach, which once characterized education systems in several Western European countries.

Although the Ministry of Education has adopted enhanced school autonomy as an offical policy, it maintains many elements that reflect a centralized educational system. In recent years sustained efforts in policy development have been made to decentralize authority and empower regional districts, local authorities, and schools. Typically, these developments have been achieved through devolution of the Ministry's traditional basic authority to direct national and social values. The introduction of the Self-Managing Schools program is a central policy effort in this direction.

It should not be assumed from the summary presentation in this chapter that with the introduction of the Self-Managing Schools program, the elementary and junior high schools in Israel have shifted dramatically from an extreme of external centralized Ministry control to a position of entirely unfettered autonomy. In reality, for several years schools enjoyed various degrees of autonomy before the Self-Managing Schools program was initiated. However, prior to the introduction of the new program, the provision of limited school autonomy was not framed within official, legal, or formal legislation and was implemented in an inconsistent manner. Some schools had acquired a degree of independence as a result of earlier success and achievement—especially those that enjoyed positive leadership and the support of parents and the local authority—such as a number of distinguished community schools. Others gained degrees of autonomy over their functioning because the local inspector was too busy to become involved in the internal operation of the school or was simply reluctant to do so because of a variety of constraints.

In addition, many educators believe that schools in Israel have had extensive pedagogical autonomy for many years resulting from the absence of systematic, standardized testing until grade 12, and the freedom to determine locally developed curricula for up to 25 percent of the instructional time available in schools. Although external examinations for different grades were introduced in the early 1990s, they were discontinued shortly thereafter following extensive debate that raised such issues as teaching to the tests, excessive public accountability, the impact of public comparison of schools' performance, and arguments over public rights to specific information about schools.

Efforts to provide schools with greater autonomy were made during the 1970s and 1980s but with only limited success. Inbar's article "Is it Possible to Have Autonomy in a Centralized School System?" (1989) reviews the limitation of the centralized system in Israel and evaluates past efforts to decentralize authority to school and classroom levels. In this view, the efforts have not been successful because those who hold the power, including inspectors and their managing supervisors, have been reluctant to relinquish hierarchial power and the right to control school policies, plans, and activities.

A major effort to change the status quo was signaled in 1992 through the establishment of a Steering Committee for the Self-Management of Schools by the Minister of Education. At the conclusion of its deliberations in 1993, the committee's recommendations made it clear that a self-managing school was *not* an independent school free to chart its own course (Ministry of Education and Culture, 1993). Its definition was that a self-managing school is one that acts within the framework of national goals and, where available, priorities established by local authorities and responds to the declared needs of students and the community it serves. The committee recommended that schools should operate as closed financial systems with budgets based on a per capita pupil allocation formula. The formula for resource allocation to schools should be published to demonstrate equitable treatment. The formula should also be differentiated to reflect the special needs of specific student categories or groupings. The committee also recommended that the role of the inspector require major modification to provide foci for the provision for professional advice and assistance to schools to facilitate the development of individual school forward planning *within its own priorities.* Inspectors should provide advice on ways in which goals selected by schools might be achieved.

Unsurprisingly, the committee's recommendations proved highly controversial. The main argument advanced in opposition to the recommendations was that developing power from the government to the schools would erode the concept of equality of opportunity for students—the main ethos of the Israeli education system. At many public meetings, as well as through letters to the Minister of Education, newspaper articles, and television and radio programs, concerned citizens, reporters, and experts expressed their views about the implications of the recommendations.

Opposition to the systemic change was typically reflected in partisan slogans and headlines such as: "the privatization of education," "the end of government control," "the penetration of market principles into education," and "the end of Zionism." Teachers' professional associations were opposed to the establishment of management committees (governing bodies) for schools because, in their view, such committees would diminish the status of school principals and, in turn, undermine the professional authority of teachers. Similarly, some local authorities viewed the committee's recommendations as a conspiracy on the part of the ministry to reduce status and remove power at local government level. Generally, these antipathetic reactions to reform of education in Israel were similar to those expressed in response to school reform in England and Wales during the late 1980s.

It was agreed to establish a model for the implementation of systemic reform through a national pilot project. However, some of the committee's recommendations were discarded. For example, the requirement that each school should establish a management committee was abandoned. The model identified for implementation consisted of five central elements, drawn from findings on effective schools and other school reforms:

- Identifying clear and focused goals
- Developing educational plans that were in accordance with the defined goals
- Implementing a monitoring and an assessment system
- Broadening school authority in personnel matters
- Strengthening school independence in the areas of budgetary management

An important element missing from the list was the involvement of parents as partners in the educational process. This factor, recognized as a major element in educational reform throughout developed countries, was identified during the process of the selection of those schools for participation in the pilot project. When the Self-Managing Schools pilot project was launched in 1995, seven of the nine participating schools were designated community schools.

A further thirty-four schools were added in 1996 to form an expanded Self-Managing Schools program consisting of forty-three schools distributed across a total of fifteen municipalities. While in the first group a large majority of the schools were community schools, only 50 percent of the schools selected for the second group were in the community school category.

The expansion of the pilot project offered further insights into the implementation of the program in different school environments. It became evident that when a local authority operates the majority of its schools under a centralized model, it tends to treat a pilot project self-managing school in its jurisdiction as an exception and to address the requirements of the new provision inconsistently. It is only when consideration is being given to the expansion of the program to the majority or all the schools in the authority that a comprehensive, more meaningful revision of the financial operation becomes essential. In the expanded project the introduction of new procedures was required for administering resource allocation to schools and monitoring the expenditure of funds by schools.

When the city of Jerusalem, with its seventy-four elementary and junior high schools, decided to enter the self-managing program in 1997, the entire financial procedure for school operation within the city was reorganized. In Jerusalem, the transition is designed to occur over a three-year period and will include all the elementary and junior high schools. Nineteen schools participated in the first year, thirty-five were added in the second year and the remaining twenty schools are expected to participate in the project in its third year of operation. The model designed for schools in Jerusalem was somewhat different from the limited decentralization offered by the other local authorities. Funds for municipal services including water, electricity, minor renovations, maintenance, and municipal initiatives were all aggregated and distributed to schools based on the number of students. Schools in "high needs" neighborhoods are provided with additional resources. It is anticipated that the formula for allocating funds to schools in Jerusalem will be revised in future years to reflect changing variables such as economies of scale, additional support for small schools, space utilization, and any exceptional physical condition in existing buildings. An existing nonprofit organization associated with the city of Jerusalem was assigned to manage school financial accounts—principally to avoid operating within the city's cumbersome bureaucratic procedures.

Two important components are worth noting in the implementation process of the self-managing program: the research and evaluation activities geared to the different stages of implementation, and the in-service training of various staff members affected by fundamental change. The Ministry of Education invited tenders to undertake research activities that would follow the implementation of the different elements of the project program. The Scold Institute for Research in Behavioral Sciences was chosen to provide relevant information to enable detailed examination of the model and provide insights into implementation processes. Exceptionally, the type of research required was not the traditional one of testing hypotheses or examining the implementation against a detailed plan. Rather it was necessary to monitor project implementation closely in relation to the purpose of developing a practicable process, to offer constructive criticism, to identify successful activities, and make suggestions—all to facilitate the process of evolving a distinctive and effective Israeli model for self-managing schools.

The Zipper Center for Community Education was invited to provide the necessary in-service training of the staff affected by the transition to self-managing schools. This well-established center focuses on extensive learning, guidance, counseling, development, and research activities. One of its central goals is to bridge gaps between theoretical concepts and experiential practice through offering a variety of programs in areas such as community, social, and cultural leadership. The center accepted the ministry's invitation to provide the necessary training to those involved in the transition to self-managing schools—principals, teachers, secretaries, inspectors, consultants, parents, and managers of education and finance departments in local authorities—to facilitate the creation of a new culture in the development of a self-managing school system (Habinski, 1997).

Two private companies were awarded contracts to provide the ministry with information about the amounts and sources of funds made available or spent on behalf of the schools. The information, which was not readily available in consolidated form before the launch of the schools' self-managing project, provided data on per capita student expenditure from the three main sources: the government, the local authority, and the parents. The data proved to be very important in pinpointing deficiencies in the availability of resources among schools within the jurisdiction of individual local authorities and revealed even greater differentiation among schools in different local authorities.

Following the first and second years of operation of the nine schools, these and other findings reported by the Scold Institute proved to be very positive. In addition, the report revealed many of the changes in the work environment of principals. For example:

• *Most principals expressed satisfaction with the initial pilot project.* They believed their skills and knowledge associated with concepts of self-management had been enhanced and that they were more self-confident as professionals. The principals attributed much of their development as school leaders to professional training programs provided for them and their staff at the Zipper Center. Influential programs included topics such as schools as organizational cultures, relationships between the school and its broad environment, economic perspectives and school budgets, school planning sequence from vision to the achievement of goals, monitoring of progress, and evaluation of outcomes, accountability, and empowerment. In addition, each school was guided by its community school consultant, who participated in the professional development activities.

- *Significant and positive changes occurred in the working relationships between the schools and their local authorities.* Following interaction and discussion, administrative procedures and financial reporting mechanisms were simplified.

- *School authority and participation in personnel matters were extended and included the employment of additional support staff.* Inspectors of schools in the pilot project indicated their support of the appointment of new staff made by school principals. Nevertheless, principals felt their authority was severely constrained over teaching personnel—a reflection of legal difficulty in terminating the employment of teachers who are regarded as inadequate.

- *There was an enhanced feeling of independence and the stimulation of new challenges.* About 75 percent of the teachers expressed the view that their school had become more autonomous than in the previous year and 43 percent of the teachers stated they had received new assignments during the year. A significant majority of teachers (86 percent) expressed high levels of satisfaction with their roles and team working at their schools. They also indicated (an average of 4.72 out of 5 respondents) that they had considerable autonomy in pedagogical decisions related to the implementation of educational programs—for example, over classroom management or evaluation of student achievement.

- *Project schools received direct allocation of specific resources that under the former centralized system had been controlled either by the local authority or the Ministry of Education.* Unprecedentedly, school budgets included funds for professional development days and inservice training, employment of teacher substitutes, and special funding for administration, maintenance, and minor renovations of self-managing schools.

It was evident from experience gained from the initial project that participating principals and staff, who had invested considerable effort to develop their schools through the principles of self-management, experienced major and professionally stimulating innovation. For example, the increased workload at principal level left little choice other than to discard traditional ways of school operation, thus releasing the considerable and remarkable potential latent talent existing among the school staff, parents, students, and the community.

Prestine (1991) discusses the emerging role of school principals and suggests three key elements:

- Power sharing
- Participation without domination
- Facilitation

All three groups of variables are significant in the creation of an environment in which each member of the team feels a sense of partnership in the enterprise. In this context the principal's role is to create feelings of ownership and belonging, to develop the school as an enjoyable place to belong to and contribute to its mission and achievements. Under these circumstances, the role of the principal changes from a site operator who assigns tasks to teachers to one with a broad perspective in managing available human and physical resources through an ability to motivate staff to maximize their contribution in the achievement of the goals of the school (see Table 7.1).

In a context more specific to school-based management, Wohlstetter and Briggs (1994) list the "emerging roles" of the principal. They suggest three major areas:

- Designer and champion of involvement structure—works by developing and empowering decision-making teams.
- Motivator and manager of change—works by encouraging staff development.
- Liaison with the outside world—works by bringing the school new ideas about teaching and learning.

As shown in Table 7.2, the transition from one mode of operation to another cannot be a simple process. To shift from the implementation of an external policy through acts, regulations, and

Table 7.1 Planning Aspects: External Versus Internal Locus of Control

Subject	External Management	Internal Management
Planning framework vision	• A vision of the inspector, the principal, or the management committee • Limited or no involvement of the staff in shaping the vision and no intention to realize it	• A common vision • Staff and partners are committed to realize the vision
Goals and targets	• External financial resources are significant components in setting goals • A large number of goals, usually vague and general • Clients receive predetermined services • Client views not sought	• Goals are set according to what the school needs and can afford • A small number of goals that are clear and focused • Clients' needs drive priorities • Client views are considered during the process of goals setting
Monitoring and evaluation	• Emphasis on external standardized testing • Outcomes and results are not used in the development of future plans	• Greater emphasis on internal evaluation • Outcomes and results inform future plans

procedures to an operation in which the principal as leader builds teams and creates partnerships, recognizing that he or she does not have all the answers and is not an expert in every function related to school operation, requires extensive preparation. The principals in Israel were selected for their positions on criteria involving evidence of strong leadership and an ability to direct implementation of centralized policies. Now they are expected to change their mode of operation and reflect the new expectations of principals of self-managing schools.

Table 7.2 Experience: External Versus Internal Locus of Control

Subject	External Management	Internal Management
1. Ministry of Education	• Manages the principal and staff	• Serves as a professional and economic resource to the principal and staff
	• The system is at the center and the principal serves it	• The school is at the center and the system's responsibility is to create the optimal conditions for the school's success
	• The ministry is responsible for the teachers' professional development program and determines its content	• The school determines the professional development activities of the staff
	A bureaucratic model	A decentralized model
	• Hierarchical structure	• Flat structure
	• Many directives, rules, and regulations	• Limited directives, rules, and regulations
	• Emphasis on standardization	• Emphasis on differentiation
2. School	• Semi-closed system	• Open system
	• Acts on the basis of external directives that usually do not encourage interaction with with the environment	• Defines its direction on the basis of interaction with its environment
	• Encouragement and criticism come from the inspector	• Encouragement and criticism come from the local environment (students, staff, parents)
a. Principal's Status and Role	• Follows directions	• Undertakes general responsibility
	• Implements and directs implementation	• Manages human resources
	• Messenger	• Team builder

(continued)

Table 7.2. *(continued)*

Subject	External Management	Internal Management
	• Arbitrator, mediator	• Facilitator
	• Activates staff	• Empowers others
(Accountability)	"I do what I am told to . . . someone else is to blame."	"I take personal responsibility for the results."
	"If they only enabled us . . . "	"The buck stops here."
b. Teacher	• A teacher's job and responsibilities begin and end with direct instruction and assigned chores	• A teacher leads a self-managing class and has a broad view of the needs of the school and its clients
	• Partner, decision maker, determines required support services	• Employee, follows instructions
c. Parents	• Expected only to participate in fund-raising activities	• Active partners who take responsibility in support of student learning
	• Are considered "out of bounds," external, not a partner	• Support and assist the school
	• Receive information on their child's progress	• Are clients whose feedback is valued
3. Mode of operation	• Domination of external initiative	• Initiatives reflect local needs and priorities
	• A large number of projects	• Selective choice of projects
	• Difficult to limit goals and set local priorities	• Number of goals is limited to what is possible to achieve and reflects local priorities
	• Schools are reluctant to decline projects because of the resources attached	• Schools do not depend on external projects for financial needs
	• Limited school initiatives	• New school initiatives as a way of life

Subject	External Management	Internal Management
Information	• Information about resources, initiatives, and projects is restricted	• Information about resources and initiatives is open, accessible, and available
	• Lack of information forces short-term planning	• Available information enables longer-range planning
Funding	• Earmarked funds	• Block funds
	• Funds are allocated on a discretionary basis	• Funds are allocated based on criteria
	• Limited or no flexibility in the use of the funds	• Flexibility in the use of the funds
	• Information on the allocation of funds to schools is not public	• Information on allocation of funds to schools is made public

Conclusion

The Israeli education system was created following the establishment of the state in 1948. During the 1950s and 1960s there were strong pressures to address the urgent needs for schooling of the rapidly growing young population that arrived in massive waves of immigration. At that time, it was determined that a centralized system was the most appropriate approach to provide for equality of access to education, to build schools, to prepare teaching staff, and to develop curriculum and learning materials. Schools in the system were expected to implement policies and regulations established by central government. During the early 1970s there were calls for enhanced school autonomy and flexibility as ways of addressing growing frustration among teachers. Initial efforts to enhance school autonomy were unsuccessful due largely to the reluctance of those with power and influence to empower schools and lose control.

The self-managing school program, developed following extensive committee work, was introduced in nine pilot schools in 1995 and expanded to a total of forty-three schools in the following year. In 1997, it was decided to transfer all the elementary schools in Jerusalem to the self-managing program over a three-year period. Research undertaken in the schools that entered the program in 1995 points to a high level of satisfaction among principals both with the concept and the acquisition of skills and knowledge during professional development sessions. Other findings provide evidence of enhanced school relations with local authorities and a simplification of financial reporting mechanisms. In addition, a significant majority of teachers expressed satisfaction with their changing roles and expansion in teamwork at their schools.

The current work with the schools emphasizes enhanced activities at school level using development planning procedures. The process includes joint vision and goal setting, development of plans to achieve the declared goals, and establishment of a monitoring system to enable evaluation of outcomes in relation to achievement of goal expectations. Other areas where progress is anticipated is at the systemic level, where the respective roles and responsibilities of a school principal and an inspector require new delineation, clarification, and formal adoption.

An increasing number of local authorities have expressed interest in expanding school-based management to schools within their jurisdiction. Nonetheless, it is too early to predict whether the central authority and other local authorities would be willing to devolve power to schools and thereby change the locus of control in the Israeli education system.

References

Habinski, A. *Self-Managing Schools.* (In Hebrew.) Jerusalem: Zipper Center for Community Education. 1997.

Inbar, D. "Is It Possible to Have Autonomy Within a Centralized School System?" In I. Friedman (ed.), *Autonomy in Education.* (In Hebrew.) Jerusalem: Scold Institute, 1989.

Ministry of Education and Culture. *The Compulsory Education Law.* (In Hebrew.) Jerusalem: State of Israel, 1949.

Ministry of Education and Culture. *Regulations of State Education (Inspection Orders).* (In Hebrew.) Jerusalem: State of Israel, 1956.

Ministry of Education and Culture. *Report of the Committee on Promoting Educational Initiatives.* (In Hebrew.) Jerusalem: State of Israel, 1972.

Ministry of Education and Culture. *Recommendations of the Steering Committee for Self-Managing Schools.* (In Hebrew.) Jerusalem: State of Israel, 1993.

Ministry of Education and Culture. *A Thousand Flowers Will Bloom: An Anatomy of Activating Projects in Schools.* (In Hebrew.) Jerusalem: State of Israel, 1997.

Prestine, N. "Completing the Essential Schools Metaphor: Principal as Enabler." Paper presented at the annual meeting of the American Educational Research Association, Chicago, 1991.

State Comptroller. *Report Number 44 for the Year 1993.* (In Hebrew.) Jerusalem: State of Israel, 1994.

Wohlstetter, P., and Briggs, K. L. "The Principal's Role in School-Based Management." *Principal,* 1994, Nov.

AMI VOLANSKY *is director of the Policy Planning Division of the Ministry of Education, Jerusalem, and a lecturer at Tel-Aviv University.*

AVI HABINSKI *is managing director, monitoring and planning, Edmonton Public Schools (in Alberta, Canada) and is on sabbatical leave with the Israeli Ministry of Education.*

Index

Back Issue/Subscription Order Form

Copy or detach and send to:
Jossey-Bass Inc., Publishers, 350 Sansome Street, San Francisco CA 94104-1342

Call or fax toll free!
Phone 888-378-2537 6AM-5PM PST; Fax 800-605-2665

Back issues: Please send me the following issues at $25 each.
(Important: please include series initials and issue number, such as SL8.)

1. SL _____

_____

_____

$ _____ Total for single issues

$ _____ Shipping charges (for single issues *only;* subscriptions are exempt from shipping charges): Up to $30, add $5^{50} • $30^{01}–$50, add $6^{50} $50^{01}–$75, add $7^{50} • $75^{01}–$100, add $9 • $100^{01}–$150, add $10 Over $150, call for shipping charge.

Subscriptions   Please ❏ start   ❏ renew my subscription to *New Directions for School Leadership* for the year 19___ at the following rate:

❏ Individual $52   ❏ Institutional $105
NOTE: Subscriptions are quarterly, and are for the calendar year only. Subscriptions begin with the spring issue of the year indicated above. For shipping outside the U.S., please add $25.

$ _____ Total single issues and subscriptions (CA, IN, NJ, NY and DC residents, add sales tax for single issues. NY and DC residents must include shipping charges when calculating sales tax. NY and Canadian residents only, add sales tax for subscriptions.)

❏ Payment enclosed (U.S. check or money order only)

❏ VISA, MC, AmEx, Discover Card #_____ Exp. date_____

Signature _____ Day phone _____

❏ Bill me (U.S. institutional orders only. Purchase order required.)

Purchase order #_____

Name _____

Address _____

_____

_____

Phone_____ E-mail _____

For more information about Jossey-Bass Publishers, visit our Web site at:
www.josseybass.com   **PRIORITY CODE = ND1**